**THE AMAZING STORY
OF LEO MESSI**

THE FLEA

To Lisa & the Kids
Liz, Nick, Maddy, Emily,
and Matthew

Also by Michael Part

Cristiano Ronaldo – The Rise of a Winner

Neymar – The Wizard

THE AMAZING STORY
OF LEO MESSI

THE FLEA

MICHAEL PART

DINO

Published by Dino Books,
an imprint of John Blake Publishing Ltd,
3 Bramber Court, 2 Bramber Road,
London W14 9PB, England

www.johnblakepublishing.co.uk

www.facebook.com/johnblakebooks 🔲
twitter.com/jblakebooks 🔲

First published in this edition in paperback in 2014
First published by Sole Books in April 2013

ISBN: 978-1-78219-981-6

British Library Cataloguing-in-Publication Data:

A catalogue record for this book is available from the British Library.

Design by www.envydesign.co.uk
Cover illustration by Dan Leydon
Background image Shutterstock

Printed in Great Britain by CPI Group (UK) Ltd

9 10

Papers used by John Blake Publishing are natural, recyclable products made from
wood grown in sustainable forests. The manufacturing processes conform to the
environmental regulations of the country of origin.

TABLE OF CONTENTS

ACKNOWLEDGEMENTS

Leo Messi's is a life made in heaven and straight out of the movies. This book exists solely because of Yitzhak and Yonatan Ginsberg of Sole Books. Their devotion to the beautiful game and their love of Leo Messi rubbed off on me. Their steadfast, unconditional love and support for me made this book possible.

And to Grand Master Mark Cox for helping me think like a champion.

BARCELONA, MARCH 2001

'Flight 7767 to Buenos Aires, Argentina, is ready to board.'

The Barcelona Airport loudspeaker startled thirteen-year-old Lionel Messi and he pressed tight against his mother, Celia's, side. His father, Jorge, was next to him. Leo, as most everyone called him, would now be living in Barcelona with his father. The rest of his family – his mother, Celia, his older brothers, Matias and Rodrigo, and his baby sister, Maria Sol – were returning home to Rosario in Argentina. Leo was about to join the youth academy of the legendary football club, FC Barcelona. Those who loved the team called it by its nickname: Barça.

Today, the Messi family was splitting up for what would be a long time.

A long line of passengers began boarding the plane to Argentina. Celia kissed her husband Jorge goodbye, fighting back tears. She did not know if she could bear being without her youngest son, Leo. FC Barcelona thought he was special and she was very proud of him. If only his grandmother could have witnessed this moment. It was Grandma Celia who started it all. She was the first one to see Leo's talent.

The Messi family loved the beautiful game. And when Celia squeezed her husband's hand one last time before she boarded the plane, she remembered the football match they attended the day of their honeymoon. She turned from Jorge and hugged her son Leo, her eyes filling with the tears she could no longer hold back. 'Don't cry, Mama,' Leo said.

'I'm sorry, Leo,' she said. 'I'm being silly.'

'No, you're not, Mama,' Leo comforted. 'You just care about us.'

They had waited a long time for word from Barça. For months she had worried the team was going to do what all the other teams had done – walk away at the last minute. But instead they had chosen him and she was going home.

'We'll come home when the season is over, Mama,' Leo comforted her, wiping her tears with his hand. 'I promise.'

After months in Barcelona, hoping for Leo's success on the FC Barcelona pitch, the team had finally committed to bringing the teenager into their Academy. It was bittersweet for Celia, Matias, Rodrigo, and even little Maria Sol. They were homesick for their country, Argentina, and their town, Rosario, and they understood that this was Leo's chance to make his dreams come true and play professional football. But they loved Leo with all their hearts and would miss him terribly. He was only thirteen.

Jorge and Leo rode back to their hotel in silence. The Barça driver, Octavio, took a shortcut. Leo sat up front with him and enjoyed every minute of the ride. Jorge begged him to slow down in Argentinian Spanish and Octavio chuckled at the words he used.

He was originally from Argentina and knew the difference between Argentine Spanish and Catalan, the Spanish spoken in Barcelona.

'Did I say something funny?' Jorge asked.

'The words are different in Argentina and Catalan. Do not worry, Mr Messi. You'll learn as time goes by.

The city of Barcelona was huge and beautiful compared to Rosario, with buildings that reached up into the sky. Leo watched the skyline flash by and Jorge watched Leo. Finally, Jorge said, 'I miss them already.'

'Me too,' Leo said, his eyes glued to the scenery.

'Are you going to be able to handle this? Alone in Barcelona?'

'I won't be alone, Papa. I'll have you and I'll have the team.'

Jorge smiled, satisfied. That was one thing about Leo. He always managed. He wrapped an arm around his son and Leo leaned against him as he always did and closed his eyes. Before he dozed off, Leo thought about his dear hometown of Rosario, and how he got to Barcelona.

CHAPTER 1

FIRST BALL AND FIRST TOUCHES

The Messi family gathered around their old kitchen table in Rosario, talking excitedly. Celia had put their fancy linen tablecloth on. There was a big homemade birthday cake in the middle with four candles on it. Today, Lionel Messi was four years old, but he was nowhere to be seen. He hid behind Matias and Rodrigo, his older brothers, embarrassed, as they all sang a birthday song to celebrate him. Leo did not like all the attention, but if he did not show his face soon, he knew he would not get any cake or his present. When it came time to blow out the candles, Rodrigo looked down at his baby brother and grinned, then shoved him forward. 'Go on, make a wish, Leo,' he said.

Leo started to speak and Matias covered his mouth. 'Not out loud or it won't come true.' Leo looked up at his older brother and nodded, then squeezed his eyes tight and made his wish, moving his lips. Jorge grinned.

That is when Grandma Celia walked into the room. When Leo finished, he opened his eyes and lit up when he saw his Grandma. She was hiding his birthday present behind her back. First, she brought out one of her hands, and it was empty. Then the other and Leo immediately saw what she was holding. 'Is this what you wished for, Leo?' she asked.

'Yes!' Leo shouted with excitement as Grandma Celia tossed him a brand new football. How did she know? It was perfect: size 5 with blue pentagons. *The* classic ball. Blue was his favourite colour, everyone in the family knew that. He tucked the ball under his arm and started to dart off towards the door to play in the streets, but Matias grabbed him by the collar and yanked him back. 'Whoa,

Tiger! You can play later. Let's have some cake.'

Leo looked up at his big brother and nodded as everyone around him laughed. He laughed too as his mum cheerfully cut the cake into big squares and passed the first piece to Leo. 'For the birthday boy,' she said. Leo took the slice and munched it hungrily. It was sweet with raspberry and vanilla, just the way he liked it.

Later, Matias and Rodrigo went outside to play a game with their cousins. Leo stayed in the house. He rushed into the bedroom and peered out from under a shade at the street where his cousins and brothers played a pickup game of football. The *potrero,* the word for street in Rosario, was hot and dusty. Leo watched the boys intently, but was too shy to join them. He was much smaller than the others and figured as long as he was not among them, he could not be trampled.

'Go on, Leo,' a voice said from the doorway. Leo, who was lying on the bed, flipped around as Grandma Celia stepped into the small room.

'Go out in the *potrero* and play with the other

boys, Leo,' his grandma said. 'Don't stay cooped up in your room. You need the sun. It will help you grow.' With that, she took his wrist and pulled him to his feet. 'Come. Give your cousins some grief. Show them that you're better than those amateurs,' said Grandma Celia.

'And you can be my coach!' Leo said.

Grandma Celia chuckled as Leo snatched up his new blue ball, kissed her on the cheek, and ran out. Alone in the room, Celia scanned the walls where she had helped Leo tack pictures over his bed of the great Argentinian football hero, Maradona, and one of the best players of all time. In the Messi family, and throughout Argentina, Maradona was king.

Leo flattened himself against the side of the house, a few feet from the street, hiding and watching as his cousins and brothers charged around in the street, shouting and kicking up so much dust they could hardly see the ball. 'They are all so tall,' Leo thought, 'and I am so small.' He just could not bring himself to step out into the sunlight and let the others see him. No one would pick him anyway. He watched for a moment more, and then darted around to the kitchen side of the house.

He ran into Cintia, the neighbour girl. The two of them were womb twins; their mothers had the two of them in the same year in the same month and practically on the same day. They had been best friends ever since. 'Happy birthday, Leo. Why are you hiding?' she asked matter-of-factly.

'I'm not hiding,' Leo shot back quickly.

'Then what are you doing over here? The game is out there,' she said.

'What game?' Leo asked.

Cintia's eyes fell on the new blue ball he was holding. 'The game your cousins are playing in the street. Is that a new ball?'

She's reading my mind, Leo thought. Of course, he was hiding. He was afraid to play with the big boys. But he wasn't going to tell *her* that.

She took the ball from him and looked it over. 'It's nice,' she said, shoving it back at him. 'Maybe you want to practise with it.' Then she turned on her heel and walked away. Leo watched her for a moment, and then looked at the new ball in his hand.

Celia, his mother, was in the small kitchen preparing Leo's favourite dish for his birthday. It was an old dish handed down from the Italian side of the family. Her side. The Cuccittini side. Delicious fried beef topped with ham, mozzarella cheese, and marinara sauce. She swung the heavy skillet filled with chunks of beef and piles of egg noodles covered in gravy over to the stove and set it down with a THUD. She stopped for a second. What was that sound? THUD. There it was again. THUD. She turned the flame on the burner low and moved over to the window to see what was making that noise.

THUD. There was Leo, outside the kitchen window, kicking his new blue ball into the side of the house. THUD. Left foot, THUD. Right foot, THUD. When the ball popped up, he controlled it on his thigh, then brought it down without hesitation and played it back against the wall. THUD.

The noise brought Grandma Celia into the kitchen. THUD. She looked at her daughter curiously, and Leo's mum urged her over to the window for a look.

THUD. The new blue ball bounced off the wall and Leo caught it with his chest, let it fall to his feet, then expertly touched it from his right foot to his left and – THUD.

Grandma Celia turned to her daughter. 'He is afraid to play with the big boys,' she whispered. 'He thinks he is too small and not good enough. But I think he is too good to play with them. Look at that touch!'

Leo's mum looked again. THUD.

'He loves that ball. I knew he would,' Grandma Celia said with a big grin.

THUD.

CHAPTER 2

THE PIBE AND A DREAM

That night, Leo hid his new ball under the covers. When his father came in to say good night, he saw a big round lump next to Leo. 'Who's your friend?' Leo's father asked.

Leo giggled and whipped back the covers to reveal his brand new ball.

A year later, when Leo's father came into his room, Leo was waiting for him. His blue ball was next to him, all ragged and scratched up from days and days of kicking it around the rugged streets of Rosario.

'I hope you brushed the dirt off that thing before you crawled into bed with it,' Jorge said, pretending to scold him.

'All clean, Papa,' Leo lied, quickly brushing the red dirt that had fallen off the ball to the floor.

Jorge pretended not to see and sat down on the other side of the bed. 'Did you say your prayers?'

'Yes, Papa,' Leo said. 'I asked God to make me tall.'

Jorge studied his son for a moment. It hurt to hear his son talk about his small size. He felt responsible and wished more than anything that they could find a reason for it. 'Me too, Leo,' he replied, then thought of something: 'Have you ever heard any of the other boys mention the *Pibe?*' he asked.

'The Boy?'

'Yes, that is what the word means, but the legend of the *Pibe* is more than just words and their meanings. It is a boy from Argentina, who learns to play football in the streets, where only those who can dribble the ball can keep it,' Jorge continued.

'Like Maradona?' Leo asked.

'Exactly like Maradona,' Jorge answered. 'In fact, Maradona is the *Pibe* of our times.'

'Is this a story about Maradona?' Leo asked his father.

'No, son,' Jorge said softly. 'It is a story about you.'

This pleased Leo very much because it was his dream to grow up, become a professional football player, and have the great Maradona as his coach. He smiled up at his father and closed his eyes. And as Jorge continued to spin his tale, Leo drifted off to sleep and fell immediately into the best dream of his life.

This was a new dream, one Leo never had before. In it, he is five years old. He is in his neighbourhood near his house at 525 Estado de Israel Street in Rosario. He is setting up the ball in the vacant lot behind their house where they play pickup football. He immediately sees that the goalkeeper is his hero, Diego Maradona, wearing a black jersey. Maradona stands in the middle of the goal that is marked by two wooden sticks. Leo is so shocked at seeing Maradona that he stops and Maradona shouts at him, 'Don't stop, Leo! Take your shot! This is your game, Pibe!'

Leo touches the ball forward, slaloms with it glued to his left foot, fakes to the right, then shoots the ball to the left with his left foot and it flies over Maradona's head right under the crossbar and into the net!

Leo raises his hands into the air, victorious, and looks at Maradona, expecting the man to be upset that he could not block the shot. Instead, Maradona smiles.

'That was great, Leo! It was magical! La Nuestra!' Maradona says, lifting Leo up and tossing him into the air. Instead of coming down, Leo keeps floating up into the sky. He looks down at Maradona who gets smaller and smaller. He shouts one last time up to Leo, 'You are truly the Pibe!'

All fear leaves Leo when he hears Maradona say these words. Leo shouts back to him on the ground, 'I thought *you* were the Pibe!'

'I am, Leo! But you are next!' Maradona shouts through the clouds. 'You are next, Leo!'

Leo cannot believe it! He looks up at the sun as he keeps floating up through the clouds. He swims through them just as he used to pretend to swim in the bathtub, and the sun is so bright it wakes him up.

Leo was backwards on his bed, swimming through the blankets as if they were clouds and his beat up blue birthday ball was all the way across the room, under the window. It was morning. 'Amazing!' Leo shouted, and his mother and Grandma Celia came rushing into the room.

'What is amazing?' asked Grandma Celia.

'My dream! It was the best one yet!' Leo said.

'Good. You can tell me all about it on the way to Grandoli,' Grandma Celia said.

'Grandoli!' Leo shouted, leaping up from his bed, throwing the covers over Grandma Celia. 'Are we going to watch them play?'

Grandma Celia pulled the blanket off her head and straightened her hair. 'Is that what you want to do at Grandoli? Just watch?'

Leo shook his head. 'No! I want to play!' he said, his eyes wide with excitement.

'Exactly!' Grandma Celia replied.

'But,' Leo said, shaking his head. 'I can't play for Grandoli!'

'Of course you can, Leo,' Grandma Celia said. 'They don't know it yet, but they need a player like you. It's not every day you get to try out for the worst team in town!'

CHAPTER 3

THE WORST TEAM IN TOWN

'But Grandma, why would you want me to play on the worst team in Rosario?' Leo asked, kicking up some dust with his worn-out shoes, passing his ball from his right to his left, back and forth, as they walked up the street towards the Grandoli pitch. It was only a few blocks from Leo's home. The morning was hot, like most mornings in Rosario, but Leo felt there was something in the wind. Something special.

'Everyone knows Grandoli is the worst team in town,' Grandma Celia said.

'Who cares?' Leo asked. 'I just want to play.'

'Well,' Grandma Celia smiled whimsically.

'It might be good for you that they are doing so poorly.'

'Really?' Leo was confused.

'Yes. A lousy team needs a great player, right?'

'Yeah, but who?' Leo asked.

Grandma Celia smiled. 'You, Leo. They need you. They have no idea how good you are,' Grandma Celia continued. 'So we will show them.'

Leo beamed.

'I'll talk to the coach,' Grandma Celia said.

'What if he won't take me?' Leo felt a knot in his throat.

'Trust me. He will,' said Grandma Celia.

They walked along the banks of the Parana River and Leo could smell the muddy water and even the grain on the ship that was passing by, going down river to the sea from a nearby grain port. It would not be long before the pitch that was home to Grandoli FC would come into view. Leo could feel his heart beating faster. Just thinking about playing football made him feel that way.

The Grandoli Pitch was rough and bumpy.

Two teams were in the middle of a practice game, running back and forth, kicking dust as high as the ball, but for Leo, watching them play was not nearly as satisfying as playing. He gripped the chain link fence with both hands, pressed his nose through one of the holes, and never took his eyes off the ball.

'Stay here, Leo. I'm going to have a little talk with the coach,' Grandma Celia said.

'Okay, but I'm too small to play with these guys,' he replied, his eyes glued to the field. 'They're all bigger than me.'

Grandma Celia took him and looked him right in the eye. 'How many boys do you see out there?' she asked.

Leo pointed and counted. 'Eleven on one team, ten on the other,' he said.

'There you go.' Grandma Celia smiled to herself. 'One of the teams is down a player. You want to succeed, Leo?' she asked.

Leo nodded.

'You can only succeed if you don't give up. Are you going to give up?'

Leo shook his head.

Grandma Celia gave him a big smile and tousled his hair, then hurried off to see the coach. Leo watched her go and then returned his attention to the game.

Grandma Celia found Coach Aparicio on the sidelines, sweating profusely, nervously pacing back and forth. When he turned around to pace back, he found himself nose-to-nose with Grandma Celia. He tried to move around her but she blocked his path. 'Can I help you, Celia?' he sighed.

'Too bad you're down a player, Apa. Talk about making a bad thing worse,' she said.

'How do you know I'm down a player?' he asked.

'My grandson told me,' she said, pointing a finger down field along the fence.

Coach Apa followed her finger, saw where she was pointing, and raised an eyebrow in her direction. 'All I see is little Leo,' he said.

'You really don't know how bad your team is, do you?' she asked pointedly.

'Come on, Celia,' Coach Apa complained. 'Are you saying I should play *Leo?*'

'Why *not?*' Celia asked, flashing one of her famous smiles.

'Because he's too small. The rest of the boys, they're so big, they'll – *trample* him. And then I gotta put up with the crying and the cuts and the bruises – and *you.*' Coach Apa got right in her face.

But Grandma Celia was already two moves ahead of him. 'If he makes a peep I'll pull him off the pitch myself,' she said with confidence.

'They'll eat him alive,' Coach Apa pleaded, watching Leo downfield on the other side of the fence, expertly dribbling his ball.

'Have I ever lied to you, Apa?' Celia asked. Coach Apa looked her in the eye and shook his head.

'Then give him a chance. You won't regret it,' Grandma Celia countered confidently.

Coach Apa looked at her and slouched. 'I give up. I can never win with you, Celia.'

Grandma Celia flashed him a grin. 'You just did.'

Coach Apa reluctantly walked Leo out on the field and assigned him to the midfield, just to keep him safe.

'No rough stuff,' Apa told the players. 'He's new.'

The team captain stepped forward. He was twice as tall as Leo. 'New? He's a baby!'

'He isn't a baby,' Apa said. 'He's just small.' He said it under his breath, making sure Leo didn't hear him. 'Now get out there and do what I said.'

The team captain nodded in agreement, charged back onto the field, and the game resumed.

Coach Apa returned to the sideline and Grandma Celia joined him once more. He looked at her and raised one eyebrow.

Out on the field, Leo just stood there, not sure what he was supposed to do. The defenders and midfielders were running every which way. He darted his eyes around and locked onto the ball. It was across the pitch near the opposite sideline. His knees shook, he was so afraid.

'Run, Leo!' Grandma Celia screamed from the sidelines. 'Get the ball!'

Leo snapped out of it, stormed across the field, and worked his way closer to the ball. But no one would pass it to him. It was as if he was invisible to his new teammates.

But Leo didn't give up. He charged through the opposition's defence and immediately began pressuring the opponent with the ball. He already knew what the other player was going to do. And as the opponent tried to play the ball through Leo's legs, Leo quickly closed the gap and took control of the ball. He took a quick look around: he was only twenty-five yards from the goal!

'Cross!' Coach Apa screamed.

Leo froze for a split second. Then the ball touched his foot and he grew calm. He stopped thinking. He knew what to do. The defenders were all over him, but he evaded them all and darted forward, the ball glued to his feet.

Coach Apa had worked his way down the fence to Grandma Celia and turned to her and pushed his cap back on his head and blew out a breath. 'Did you see that? They couldn't shake him! He is like a flea you can't get rid of!' he muttered.

Grandma Celia cocked her head when she heard this. 'Flea,' she said, grinning. 'I like that.'

The first defender, the one who lost the ball, tried to tackle him. Leo grinned. Easy. He made a slight cut to the left, then passed a second defender with a speedy dribble to the left. He could not see the fear in the goalkeeper's eyes, he was still too far away. He also did not know that the defenders were coming up fast from behind. He saw his opening and calmly sent the ball through the goalkeeper's legs, a strong left-footed strike that whooshed along the ground. He could not hear the cheering. All he could hear was his grandma shouting his name. He looked over to the stands and when he saw her, he smiled. Then he raised his two fingers in the air as if to say, 'That was for you, Grandma!'

He was too far away to see her tears of joy.

In the next twenty minutes, Coach Apa was all over the sidelines, barking orders and strategies. He looked over at the fence where he had left

Grandma Celia and she was smiling back at him. He called her over to stand next to him for the rest of the game and when Leo scored his fifth goal, clinching the win, Coach Apa was so happy he grabbed Grandma Celia and kissed her on the cheek. Each goal Leo scored that day was better than the last. Coach Apa thought, this kid plays so naturally, so effortlessly. What a genius this little flea was! Every ball that went to Leo ended up in the back of the net.

The kids were all over Leo, hugging him and cheering him on. He was overwhelmed and embarrassed. No one had ever treated him that way, especially kids he did not know.

★ ★ ★

After the game, Leo came over to be with his Grandma Celia and Coach Apa and they were suddenly surrounded by other parents and spectators, all congratulating Apa on his new discovery.

'Let's go, Leo,' Grandma Celia said. 'We have to stop off at the *mercado* on the way home.'

As Leo and his grandma walked off, Coach Apa shouted after them, 'Make sure that he shows up for practice! Tomorrow!'

'He will,' Grandma said. 'The two of us will be here at four o'clock sharp.'

Coach Apa beamed and turned to the parents surrounding him. 'I'm never taking that kid off the field!'

CHAPTER 4

SCHOOL DAYS

Leo and Cintia walked to school together and neither of them said a word for a long time. Leo had his books under one arm and his ball under the other. When they arrived at the school playground, Leo dropped the ball and dribbled it across the playground, weaving in and out of the other students before they had a chance to get out of his way.

Cintia caught up with him outside their small bungalow classroom. 'You see the way they were watching you?' she asked.

Leo shrugged. 'I was just practising.'

'They look up to you,' she said.

'You mean down *at* me,' he said, looking at his feet. 'Everyone is taller than me.'

'That's not what I meant,' she shot back with a flash of anger. However, the anger did not last long. She knew what he meant, and she knew how he felt about how tall he was and how he wanted to be as tall as everyone else, especially *her*. With that, she charged into the classroom and Leo followed and sat down behind her in the last row.

As soon as all the students were in their seats, Mrs Ferreto walked down the rows cradling a stack of tests, dropping one on each desk. 'You will have fifteen minutes to complete your test,' she said, dropping a test on Cintia's desk. 'When you finish, lay your pencils down and raise your hands. She dropped a test on Leo's desk. Leo looked up her and she smiled back at him.

Leo looked at the test. It was one page, five questions. He hoped he would know at least some of the answers. He stretched out and tapped Cintia's leg with his foot. She nodded her head. Cintia was ready too.

Mrs Ferreto marched back up to the front of the class and turned the dial on an old oven timer to 15. 'All right, class,' she said, 'Begin.'

As if they were a flock of wild birds, all the students picked up their pencils in unison and started writing. Leo stared at the test paper. He should at least be able to know the answer to the first question. Wasn't the first question always the easiest? He had no idea what the answer was so he gave Cintia a kick. It was their signal. She reached her open hand back, he put a large pink eraser in it, and she made it disappear in front of her. Moments later, she handed the eraser back, Leo turned it over, and there was the answer to the first question scrawled on it.

Ten minutes later, Cintia raised her hand and Mrs Ferreto strolled down the aisle and picked up her test with a smile, then turned on her heel and marched back up to the front of the class. More hands went up around the class. Leo waited for a few more seconds, and then raised his hand. Mrs Ferreto got to all of them, then went to the front and began the process of checking everyone's answers. 'If I have picked up your test, please do today's reading assignment,' she said. Leo sighed, pulled his worn-out reading book from his satchel, opened it, and began reading.

When the bell rang announcing the lunch hour, there was a loud crescendo of desks squeaking across the grimy linoleum floor as the students stood and filed out of the room, passing directly by Mrs Ferreto. She smiled as Cintia walked past, but when Leo tried to get past her, she grabbed him by the collar and pulled him out of the line of students leaving the classroom. 'We need to talk.'

Leo's eyes widened. When the last student left the room, she turned her attention to him. 'Excellent job on your test, Leo,' she said.

'Thanks,' he said and tried to leave, but she blocked his exit. 'I'm not finished,' she said. Leo slumped. This was it. The end of the world as he knew it. Even though he and Cintia's Pink Eraser System was perfect, Mrs Ferreto was canny and saw through their scheme. 'You did very well on the test. In fact, you and Cintia got the exact same score,' she continued, giving him her most demanding look.

He shrunk under her gaze. 'Wow, amazing,' was all he could say.

'And the exact same answers. All of them. Word for word.'

Rats! He had slipped up. He knew he was supposed to change the words so it would not look like they were cheating. But the morning was so beautiful, and he wanted to get out on the playground and kick the ball around and, more importantly, not fail the test.

'Now, I would say that either Cintia looked at your answers, or you looked at hers. It was not difficult to figure out who looked at whose, Leo. I think it was you.'

Leo's shoulders slumped and he looked at his feet because he could not look her in the eye.

'What do you have to say, Leo?' Mrs Ferreto asked.

Leo took a long time to answer, but finally the

words came out of his mouth, 'I did it. I copied off Cintia,' he confessed.

Mrs Ferreto thought about it for a moment. 'Sit down,' she said pointing him to his desk.

'Aren't you going to expel me?' Leo asked, going back to the fourth desk in the last row just behind where Cintia sits.

'No,' she said. I'm going to teach you the material *again* and then I'm going to make you take the test. *Again.* And this time, I expect you to pass it – *on your own!*'

And so, Mrs Ferreto began her lessons, this time just for Leo.

When the lunch hour was over, the students returned to the classroom, but Mrs Ferreto would not let them in. One by one, their faces appeared in the windows watching, as Leo scrawled on the paper in front of him. Finally, when he finished writing, he set his pencil down and raised his hand. Mrs Ferreto came over, picked up his test paper, and studied the answers. There were only five of them. Five new ones. It did not take her long to take a red pencil and scrawl through one of the answers. Leo was worried she was going to continue scrawling until they were all scratched out in red, but she did not. Instead, she looked at him and smiled. 'Congratulations, Leo,' she said. 'You passed.' And with that, she turned on her heel and marched back up the aisle to the front of the class and let the rest of the students in.

Leo straightened up in his seat. He could not believe it! He passed! Without Cintia or the pink eraser.

Leo and Cintia walked home together and no one said a word for a long time. Leo finally broke the silence. 'Cintia?'

'Yes?' Cintia said absently.

'I really feel a whole lot better.'

Cintia smiled at him. 'You mean, like when you score a goal?'

Leo grinned and shook his head. 'No. Nothing feels as good as scoring a goal.'

CHAPTER 5

NEWELL'S CALLING

Leo caressed the ball with his chest, let it drop to his feet, and started dribbling downfield with his left foot.

'Man on Leo!' one of the midfielders on the Grandoli team yelled. But Leo already knew the defender would be there. They were always there. When the defender finally showed, near the goal, Leo stopped, kept the ball on his right, then faked to the left, and the defender bit. Leo kicked the ball right, weaved past another defender and shot the ball over the head of the keeper, scoring his third goal for Grandoli and a hat trick for himself. He had just turned nine.

Mr Griffa, big and muscular from working his entire life, stood up with the rest of the crowd. He had never seen the Grandoli stands this full. He did not come by here much. There was no reason to. There were no geniuses coming out of the worst team in town. He sat back down and continued watching the game, hoping he wouldn't be noticed by his friend Coach Apa. He was not there on a friendly visit. He was there to see Leo Messi, who some were calling a prodigy. Like Maradona. It was important that Mr Griffa could watch the boy in peace without constant interruption, so he sat near the end of the stands even though there were plenty of seats. His eyes met Coach Apa's and he smiled. Here comes trouble.

Coach Apa wasn't the first to see Mr Griffa from the city's most famous football club, Newell's Old Boys. Matias and Rodrigo Messi were with Coach Apa and pointed him out in the stands. Coach Apa knew immediately why he was there: to wrestle Leo Messi away from him.

After two years, they were coming for The

Flea, Coach Apa thought. The kid could not have stumbled or something, he had to get a hat trick right in front of Mr Griffa. 'Why couldn't he have had a bad day?' Coach Apa said out loud, suddenly feeling sorry for himself.

Leo's father, Jorge, came alongside Coach Apa to have a look. He knew Mr Griffa quite well. Jorge had played for Newell's when he was thirteen and both of his older sons started playing there when they were seven years old. There was a lot of love in the Messi family for the Red and the Black; that is what they called Newell's Old Boys. Jorge and his two oldest sons were proud to be *Lepers,* the team nickname for what they considered the best team in town. There was a longstanding rivalry between the Lepers and the other Rosario Club, Rosario Central. But the Messis knew no other team but Newell's in their hearts.

Mr Griffa had seen enough. He got up from his seat, marched down the row, excusing himself from the other spectators, and went down the two steps to the dirt. He walked briskly along the side of the pitch until he reached Jorge and Matias. Mr Griffa motioned for the boys to come over to him. They fell all over themselves and ran to his side.

'Yes, Mr Griffa?' Matias asked.

'When you come to practice,' Mr Griffa said in a hoarse voice. 'Bring your little brother.'

'Yes sir, Mr Griffa!' said Rodrigo and shot a glance over to his father, who nodded back, pleased.

'Good day,' Mr Griffa said, walking away. He stopped and turned back. 'And thank you for inviting me.' Then he continued on his way up the bumpy road that led to Newell's Old Boys' field across town. Matias and Rodrigo looked at each other, puzzled.

When Mr Griffa was out of earshot, Matias turned to Rodrigo. 'I didn't invite him, did you?' he asked.

Rodrigo just shook his head and looked over at his father, who also shook his head. Then they all looked back up the road at Mr Griffa and at that moment Grandma Celia appeared out of nowhere and caught up to him, patted him on the back, and

talked to him animatedly. Rodrigo and Matias
tried to hear what they were saying, but they were
too far away. After a few more words, Grandma
Celia sent Mr Griffa on his way, and turned back to
them with a happy smile. When she knew the
boys and Jorge were looking, she gave them two
thumbs up.

★ ★ ★

The entryway to Malvina's, home of Newell's Old
Boys football school and youth team, was a white
washed wall with 'Es El Glorioso Newell's Old
Boys' in big bold alternating red and black letters. It
meant, 'The Glorious Newell's Old Boys.' Next to
it was a red-painted metal gate that led out to the
pitch. To get to the pitch, you had to pass through
the gate and under the welcome sign. And that's
just what Leo and Grandma Celia did.

'Leave this to me,' Grandma Celia said, taking
Leo's hand and walking him onto the pitch until
she found Gabriel Digerolamo, one of the three
coaches of Newell's Old Boys football team. The

team was already out on the pitch, practising small-sided possession drills working on keeping the ball away from the opponent making accurate short passes, followed by five-yard sprints to get into the open space. These kids were well coached and Leo could see that immediately.

'Mr Griffa said to bring Leo to practice,' Grandma Celia said. 'So here he is.'

Digerolamo looked at Leo. Dear God, he thought, he is smaller than I thought. He looked at Grandma Celia. 'He's tough?' he asked.

'Is Maradona tough?' she asked back.

Digerolamo laughed loudly at her boldness. 'Well, let's see what Little Maradona can do,' he said, and then he turned to Leo. 'What position do you play?'

'I'll play where you need me,' Leo answered, bothered by something.

Digerolamo laughed again. 'Can you score?'

'Yes, sir!' Leo said

'Good, let's start you as a right midfielder,' said the coach.

Leo nodded and started to run off to the pitch, then stopped and turned back. 'Sir?'

'Yes?' asked Digerolamo.

'I'm not little.'

Digerolamo stopped in his tracks for a moment. Maybe the kid was stronger than he thought. 'Well, what do you want me to call you?'

'My friends call me Flea,' Leo said, as he ran on to the field.

Digerolamo took his cap off and scratched his head. 'Okay, Flea,' he said. He looked at Grandma Celia and she shrugged. 'He doesn't like his size much,' she said.

'I got that,' Digerolamo said, then blew his whistle and glued his eyes to the pitch where Leo took off with the ball. He could not believe it. How did he get the ball so soon?

Digerolamo thought he must have missed something. The other coaches, Ernesto Vecchio and Carlos Morales, soon joined him. They came over but their eyes were riveted on the pitch where Leo weaved between four players as he charged onwards and fired a quick shot into the bottom left side netting. First goal at Newell's.

Leo turned after he shot the goal and half his team dived on him, bringing him to the ground. They were excited and were shouting and ruffling his hair and as soon as he got back on his feet, play resumed.

Gabriel Digerolamo, Ernesto Vecchio, and Carlos Morales all sat backwards on the bench behind them at the same time. 'Did you see that strike?' asked Morales.

'I have eyes,' said Vecchio.

'He wants us to call him Flea,' said Digerolamo.

'Flea?' asked Morales.

'But don't make fun of his size,' said Digerolamo. 'He's sensitive.'

Vecchio raised his finger and was about to say something, but just then the players erupted in cheers and there was a crescendo of shouting coming from the pitch as the team piled on Leo again. The three coaches looked up. Leo had scored another goal.

All three coaches sat back down on the bench and looked at each other. Vecchio held out his arm to Digerolamo. 'Pinch me. I think I'm dreaming,' he said.

★ ★ ★

Jorge Messi was nervous when he knocked on Coach Apa's front door. Apa was an old friend and there was no easy way to do this. And when the Grandoli coach opened the door and saw Jorge, his smile fell into a frown. 'What is it, Jorge, as if I did not know?' he asked.

'Apa, I have very good news,' Jorge blurted out.

'Good news?' Coach Apa asked, totally confused.

'Malvinas wants Leo to play for Newell's Old Boys!' Jorge said and took Coach Apa by the shoulders and shook him. 'Isn't that wonderful?'

'How could this be good news, Jorge? I had the best player in all of Rosario and now I don't,' Coach Apa said and walked back into his house.

'It is good news for Leo,' Jorge called after him.

Jorge heard Coach Apa sigh from within the shadows of the house. In a moment, he reappeared into the sunlight, nodding his head. 'You are right, my friend. It is good news for Leo. At least Grandoli's had him for a little while,' he said, accepting his fate. 'Now excuse me, I have to cry.'

Jorge burst out laughing and Coach Apa looked at his old friend. 'I'm not very good at mourning,' he said, then joined him in uproarious laughter and hugged Jorge. 'What am I saying it is good news for Leo? It is *great* news! Let's celebrate!' Coach Apa draped his arm over his friend's shoulder and walked him into the house. 'I have some beer in the fridge,' he said, then closed the door.

For a month, Leo was at Old Boys on a trial basis. He played in every game and every position on the Newell's Old Boys team, and excelled in all of them. Leo scored a total of twenty-eight goals that month.

Leo's trial period with Newell's Old Boys was up on 21 March 1994. The coaches and the owners held a meeting in the small offices at Malvinas. Leo sat on the bricks outside with his father, waiting. He shifted uncomfortably. He did not have his ball with him. Ever since he got his first ball as a gift from his Grandma Celia, he had been given a new one every birthday. It was all he ever wanted and he kept every one of them in his room. He wished he had one now. It was the only thing that helped him relax. He shifted uncomfortably and looked around and that's when he saw a small lemon tree next to the building. He trotted over to it and picked up a lemon that had fallen to the ground and returned to his seat and began dribbling the lemon with his feet. The knot in his stomach went away instantly and he smiled as he juggled the lemon easily, alternating feet. Left foot, touch. Right foot, touch.

Jorge watched, amused as his son flipped the lemon back and forth, faster and faster.

There was no glass in the windows of the Malvinas office and he could hear the men talking but he could not make out everything they were saying.

One man called him 'Mozart' and another voice spoke about how 'amazing the little guy was.'

After a few minutes, the three coaches came out of the room with big smiles on their faces, followed by the rest of the men.

Leo and his father stood up.

Coach Vecchio spoke as if he were presenting Leo with the World Cup. 'Lionel Messi,' he said, 'It is with great pleasure that I welcome you as an official member of Newell's Old Boys.' He turned and Coach Morales, who stood behind Vecchio, handed him something. Vecchio turned back and Leo could see Coach Vecchio was holding a red and black uniform in his arms. Leo's heart leaped and he dropped the lemon and immediately captured it with his feet.

The men of Malvinas laughed, recognizing Leo's dedication, and Coach Vecchio handed Leo the red and black uniform. 'Welcome to the team,' he said and shook Leo's hand.

Then another man appeared from the office. A tall man with large hands. He went straight to Jorge: 'Mr Messi, I have heard astounding things about your boy,' he said with a soft, soothing voice.

'If I may have a word with you in private?'

Jorge Messi stepped forward. 'Of course.' The tall man offered him his business card and the two of them went back inside the office.

Leo was surrounded by the men of Newell's Old Boys, patting him on the back and congratulating him. Vecchio took Leo by the shoulders. 'Let's get to work.'

CHAPTER 6

THE GOOD DOCTOR

Jorge Messi bounded into Leo's room and shook him awake.

Leo sprung awake and cried out, covering his head, thinking it was an earthquake. Then he saw his father.

Jorge had to peel his son's hands away from his head. 'I have great news, Leo!'

Leo rubbed the sleep from his eyes. 'What is it, Papa?' he asked sleepily.

'The *Lepers* have been invited to play in the Friendship Cup tournament! We are going to Lima!'

Leo sat up, wide awake. 'Peru?!'

'It is a great honour. You will be competing with

many other teams from Argentina, Chile, Ecuador, even Columbia!'

It had been a year since Leo had joined Newell's Old Boys and in that year, the *Lepers* were unstoppable. They won every game against their rivals, the *Scoundrels* of Central City, and since all the boys on Leo's team had been born in or around 1987, they were known as *The Machine of '87*. And now, *The Machine of '87* was going to Lima!

'But first things first!' Jorge said to Leo, waving the business card he had been given by the unknown gentleman at Malvinas all those months ago.

'What's first, Papa?' Leo asked.

'First we see a doctor!' Jorge said.

The next day Celia and Jorge walked up the steps to the medical building with Leo between them and went inside. The waiting room was plain and empty with a small couch on one side and a few chairs on the other. There was a table in the centre stacked with old magazines. Leo and his mum sat down on the couch and Jorge went to a short railing with a fogged sliding-glass window with a door next to it. There was a bell on the railing, Jorge pushed down on it, and it rang. Almost immediately, the fogged glass window slid open. The woman behind the glass was old with a kind face. 'Name?' she asked.

'Leo Messi,' Jorge said.

'Ah,' the woman said and quickly shut the window, leaving Jorge standing there puzzled. He turned and shrugged to his wife and son.

Leo shoved his hand in his pocket and felt the lemon he had stashed there before they left for this meeting. But just as he was about to pull it out and start dribbling, the door opened and Dr Schwartzstein came in with a smile on his face. It was the man who had given Jorge his business card the other day at Newell's Old Boys pitch. 'So happy to see you, Mr Messi,' the doctor said, pumping Jorge's hand.

Leo let go of the lemon in his pocket and politely stood up. His mum smiled at him and stood alongside him.

'Come,' said the doctor wagging his hand for Leo and Celia to come. 'So good to finally meet you, Leo.'

'Thanks,' said, Leo unsure of what to do.

'I have watched you play and I think you are very special indeed. Do you know what I do here?'

'Yes,' Leo said. 'You help kids grow.'

The doctor smiled. 'Exactly,' he said. 'There is a hormone in your body that is in charge of your growth. It is not working correctly. But you no longer need to worry, Leo. Many kids have this exact same problem, but thanks to medical science we now have ways to help this hormone do its job.'

'And make me taller?' Leo asked.

'Yes. And make you taller,' the doctor said.

Leo felt instant joy. He looked at the doctor with admiration.

★ ★ ★

Dr Schwartzstein's lab was sparse and simple. Leo sat on a patient bed and the doctor came over with a syringe. 'I am just going to take a little blood from you so I can run some tests.'

Leo nodded bravely.

'This will only sting for a second, Leo,' he said, turning Leo's arm over and carefully injecting the needle under his skin.

'I'm okay,' Leo said, grimacing as the needle went into his forearm. The doctor removed the syringe end and replaced it with a test tube and the tube filled with Leo's blood. Celia took Leo's hand, just in case.

Jorge quickly looked up at the ceiling. He did not like needles.

When the tube could hold no more, the doctor pulled the needle and tube out and applied pressure while he placed a small bandage on the pinprick. 'There! That wasn't so bad, was it?'

'No sir,' Leo said. 'It didn't hurt at all.

'I knew the first time I saw you play, that you were a very brave boy. The other team, they would always try to tackle you and bring you down, but you never gave in and you always stayed on your feet, even when they hit you from behind. And when you did go down, you never complained. When I saw this, I knew you were remarkable!' Leo blushed. It was great hearing what the doctor had to say about him, but it embarrassed him.

'And I noticed something else,' the doctor said. 'You don't dive for fouls or penalties.'

'Leo would never fake being hurt. *Ever.*' Jorge explained, still staring at the ceiling.

The doctor just shook his head in wonderment. 'Good,' he finally said. 'Oh. And you can look now, Mr Messi.'

Jorge warily lowered his eyes from the ceiling and blew a breath of relief when he saw the needle had been removed.

'I will let you know the results as soon as we can finish the tests,' Dr Schwartzstein said to Celia and Jorge as he walked the three of them out to the front of the building.

'Thank you, Dr Schwartzstein,' Jorge said. 'I can't tell you how much we appreciate what you are doing for us.'

'I'm just doing my job,' the doctor replied, flashing a big smile. Then he turned without another word and went back into his office.

★ ★ ★

The 13th annual Friendship Cup tournament in Lima, Peru, was over 1,800 miles from Rosario. Sixty-eight hours by bus or three hours by plane. The Newell's Old Boys team had played magnificently all year and had earned a place in the tournament.

★ ★ ★

The Newell's Old Boys staff and players stayed with various families around the tournament locale in Lima and Leo and Jorge were no exception. They stayed with the Mendez family, whose own son, Kewin, played for Cantolao, one of the opposing local teams.

The pitch in Lima was smooth and flat, nothing like the fields in Rosario, which were more like mountaintop meadows than well-groomed pitches.

Newell's Old Boys won their match right out of the
gate at the Friendship Cup Tournament and went
on to win all their games. They rapidly advanced
through the tournament and into the finals where
they faced off against Cantolao. *The Machine of '87*
had made it to the top. Thousands of fans at the
Friendship Cup were getting their first look at the
wizard from Rosario, young ten-year-old Leo Messi,
but no one was prepared for what they were about
to see in the game against Cantolao.

Leo stood at the top of the stands looking down
at the field where he had already scored five goals
in the first half of the game. The halftime at these
matches was usually nothing more than a chance
for the fans to buy food or go to the bathroom. This
time Leo was going to keep them in their seats.
Leo started dribbling through the stands, working
his way down to the pitch, playing his favourite
ball exercise: 'keepy-uppy' where he kept the ball
in the air bouncing it off alternating knees then
insteps and finally his laces. No one in the stands
moved as he travelled through them, past children

and adults. They could not take their eyes off him.

Leo smiled and nodded to the fans as he moved down the rows towards the pitch, the ball never touching the ground. They shouted at him, 'Go Leo!' and slapped his hand as he passed them by, showing them things they had never seen before, finally jumping to the dirt and sprinting off towards the team seats, dribbling the ball.

The crowd in the stands leaped to their feet, applauded, and cheered wildly. Leo turned, just before he left the pitch, and waved to them, then ran off and vanished into the throng of Newell's Old Boys, who surrounded him and piled on him with affection.

In the second half of the game, Leo scored three more goals and *The Machine of '87* took the final game against Cantolao 10–0 and won the championship. After the game, Kewin Mendez came over to Leo with a big smile on his face. 'No one has ever scored eight goals in one game before,' he said, 'Not here, not ever.' He offered Leo his hand and Leo shook it. 'You are like Maradona,' Mendez said.

Then he asked, 'How do you do it?'

'Do what?' Leo asked.

'This. The way you play? Who taught you?'

Leo didn't answer. He scratched his head. People had asked him this question before but he never knew how to answer them. It embarrassed him.

'I don't know,' he finally said. 'I learned with these.' He pointed to his eyes. 'And I live to play.' Then he just shrugged and grinned at his new friend.

With that, he pulled off his jersey and gave it to the boy, then charged off to join the rest of his team.

Kewin Mendez gripped the red and black number 10 jersey tightly as he watched his friend leave. He vowed to himself that he would keep it with him for the rest of his life to remember the boy who stayed with him on those few hot summer days during the Friendship Cup; the boy who created magic with a ball.

CHAPTER 7

ANSWERS

Leo was out of breath by the time he reached the top of the hill. Although it was only a few blocks from his house, it was the country and it was peaceful and he could no longer hear any cars or trucks. He sat down under an olive tree and blew out a breath. He needed to think. This was his secret spot. When he had a question about what to do, he always came here to get the answer. He didn't know how it worked, only that it worked. He wasn't there more than a couple minutes before Cintia ambled up.

'Why are you here?' Cintia asked, kneeling down beside him, careful not to dirty her school dress.

'It is so quiet and I am deciding which team I want to play for: Newell's or Barcelona? What do you think?' he said, matter of factly.

'Are you kidding? You came all the way up here to daydream?' she asked. She wasn't buying it.

'I want to be as great as Maradona,' he said.

'Of course you do,' she said. 'Why are you *really* here, Leo?'

Leo was irritated. How did she know?

'You didn't climb all the way up here to your secret spot just to daydream. You can do that on a bus bench.'

Leo let out a breath. 'Okay. The doctor is going to tell us about the tests. Mama and Papa are very nervous. Me too. So I came up here.'

'To hide,' Cintia said, stretching out her legs and putting her hands behind her head.

'Maybe,' Leo replied.

'Why? Do you think it is going to be bad news? Why can't it be good news?'

Leo thought about it a long time and did not say a word. Cintia waited patiently and watched the clouds roll by. Finally, Leo said, 'You're right. I'm scared.'

'Me too, Leo,' she soothed. 'What do the *Lepers* teach you when you are facing off against an opponent?'

'Face my fears,' Leo answered without hesitation.

'Right!' Cintia said and smiled and got to her feet. She reached out her hand and Leo took it and she pulled him to his feet. 'I'm glad we had this conversation,' she said and turned and started walking down hill. Leo grinned. He came here to hide from answers and to find answers and he got them both. He ran after her and they both walked down the mountain together.

★ ★ ★

Leo fidgeted in the metal chair in Dr Schwartzstein's waiting room, his ball between his feet. His mother sat across from him on the small couch, folding and unfolding her hands. His father, Jorge, stood at the window, nervously watching the cars drive by. When Dr Schwartzstein came into the room, everyone jumped at once.

'So good of you to come,' the doctor said pressing Celia's hand between his. 'Leo, congratulations on your victory in Lima!' he said.

'Thank you,' Leo said. 'Do you have good news for me?'

'As a matter of fact, I do,' the doctor said. 'I have the tests back and just as I suspected, the results point to a condition known as Growth Hormone Deficiency. We call it GHD. It sounds serious and it is, but I also want you to know that it is not only treatable, the treatment has a very high success rate. Given Leo's physical fitness, I see no reason why he can't grow to his full height potential.'

Leo brightened, more relieved than he let on. 'I will grow?'

Dr Schwartzstein smiled and draped his arm over Leo's shoulders. 'I promise.'

Celia went to Jorge and he put his arm around her and they both seemed to breathe a sigh of relief as one. 'That is indeed good news!' said Jorge.

'I am so grateful to you doctor, this is amazing,' Celia said.

Dr Schwartzstein hesitated for a brief moment and in that instant, Leo sensed there was a problem. 'What do I have to do, doctor?' he asked.

'Yes, doctor, what is the treatment?' Celia asked.

'A series of injections, every day for several years,' he replied, turning to Leo. 'You will have to inject yourself,' he said.

'I can do it,' Leo said without hesitation.

'Great. I'm sure you can.' Then the doctor turned to Jorge. 'I would like to speak with both of you in private.'

Jorge nodded. 'Leo,' he said. 'Why don't you take your ball outside, so we can speak with the doctor alone.'

'Okay, Papa,' Leo said and sprang for the door. Whenever grown-ups wanted to talk, things always got boring or confusing really fast.

'Let's talk about the cost,' the doctor said, as soon as Leo left the room. 'The treatments are very expensive.'

'*How* expensive?' Jorge asked coming closer.

'Around $1,000 to $1,500 a month,' the doctor said.

There was silence in the room. Celia looked to Jorge, her eyes pleading, desperate. That was more than he made in a month at the steel mill. They could never afford it, she thought. 'But how–,' she cut herself off. She felt as if a door was slamming on them.

The doctor finally broke the silence. 'It is a lot of money, I understand,' he said. 'But this is Argentina and there are ways.'

'What ways?' asked Jorge, irritated and scared at the same time.

'There is the Social Security Foundation and you work at Acindar Steel Mills, right?'

'Yes,' Jorge said.

'There is always a way, Mr and Mrs Messi,' the doctor said. 'Don't lose faith now. God will provide.'

Jorge hugged his wife tightly to his side. He knew this was hurting her, but he vowed he would do anything for his children. 'We won't let Leo down,' he comforted Celia. We will find a way.'

★ ★ ★

A week later, Jorge ran home from the Acindar Steel Mills as fast as he could, happily waving to everyone he passed. He flew down the dirt road, past the river, his feet barely touching the ground. When he got to his house on Estado de Israel, he burst in through the front door, scaring his wife and baby daughter Maria Sol. 'We got the money!' he shouted.

The entire Messi family and Grandma Celia sat around the table, munching dinner, waiting anxiously for Jorge to explain. Matias and Rodrigo and Leo and little Maria Sol on one side of the table and the grown-ups on the other. Jorge cleared his throat and there was a hint of pride in what he was about to say.

'Spit it out!' Celia shouted at him.

'The Social Security Foundation has agreed to pick up part of the bill!' he blurted out.

Everyone cheered. Everyone but Celia. '*Part* of the bill?' she asked. '*Which* part?'

'Let me finish, Celia,' Jorge said, soothing her nerves. 'The factory – Acindar – is paying the rest!'

★ ★ ★

Celia relaxed and there was more cheering around the table, but this time Leo was silent. He closed his eyes and quietly thanked God.

CHAPTER 8

THE CHAMPIONSHIP SNIFFLES

Leo sat on the couch in his living room, giving himself an injection in the leg. Matias and Rodrigo stood nearby, watching their little brother, horrified. 'I don't think I could do that,' Matias said.

'You're crazy, Leo,' Rodrigo said.

Leo grinned. 'It's easy. You would do it too if it made you tall!'

'I'm already tall,' Rodrigo said. 'Besides, I hate shots.'

'Chicken,' Leo teased, finished up, expertly capped the needle, threw everything into a hazardous materials bag, and sealed it tight.

Matias and Rodrigo charged out the front door with their football duffle bags. 'See you on the pitch,' Matias said. 'Don't be late. We have an important game today.'

It had been a week since Leo started the treatments for his growth hormone deficiency and he had given himself an injection each day since Dr Schwartzstein showed him how to do it. Leo thought the little bit of pain from the needle was worth it, as long as he was going to grow as tall as the rest of the boys.

★ ★ ★

In the next two years, Leo led Newell's Old Boys to victory after victory and one championship after another. Grandma Celia sat in the same seat in the same stands for every game. One morning Leo woke up sick; not the kind of sickness that he made up to stay out of school, but a real gut-wrenching pain that made it hard to get out of bed. He woke up and instead of leaping out of bed and measuring himself to see if he had grown overnight, he just moaned.

Leo's mother, Celia, hurried into the room with a

thermometer and shoved it into his mouth without a word. She checked the thermometer after a couple of minutes. 101. He definitely had a fever. 'You're staying home,' she said and started to leave the room. 'I'll make some soup.'

'But mum!' Leo called weakly after her. 'I *can't* stay home today!'

Celia turned slowly in the doorway. She could not believe her ears. 'Let me guess. It's Saturday. And since it is not a school day, no sickness is bad enough to keep you in,' she said, raising an eyebrow.

'No. Today's the championship game,' he said, starting to get out of bed.

Leo's mum stared him down for a moment then crossed her arms. She always did this when she knew she was about to lose an argument. Everyone in the family knew it. It was her signal to them that they were about to get their own way. 'Championships!' she said with mock disgust, throwing her arms up in the air and bolting out of the room.

A short while later, Coach Vecchio stood in front of Leo. Neither of them said a word for a long time. 'Coach Vecchio, I gotta get dressed,' Leo finally said hoarsely.

'I don't know, Leo, you don't look so good,' Coach Vecchio said. He thought about it, and then placed his open palm on Leo's forehead. It was hot. Coach Vecchio had to make a tough decision. He bit his lower lip, then finally said, 'Sorry, kid. You're sick.'

'I'm not that sick, honest' Leo said, coughing and pleading. Then he said, 'Hey! If one of the guys on the other team runs into me, I can spread my germs!'

Coach Vecchio laughed and slapped Leo on the back and for that very brief moment, Leo thought he was going in. Then his coach issued a flat-out, 'No.'

Leo was crestfallen and looked down at his feet and kicked the dirt, then accepted his fate and moved off to watch the game from the sidelines.

In the first ten minutes of the game, the opposing team scored against Newell's and suddenly just like that, they were down 1–0. Leo shot a pleading glance over to Coach Vecchio, who took his time to shake his head. When another ten minutes went by and the opposing team had three more shots on goal and Newell's couldn't compose a single attack, Coach Vecchio couldn't take it anymore. He quickly turned to Leo and asked: 'How you feeling now, Flea?'

Leo was ready for him and knew exactly what to say: 'Thanks for letting me rest, Coach. I feel great now!'

Coach Vecchio eyeballed him, then nodded and wrote something on his card. Then he signalled the referee, who trotted over to him. 'I'm making a change,' he said to the ref and handed him the card. At the next stoppage, the ref looked at the card and nodded, allowing the change. A forward was coming out and Leo was going in.

Coach Vecchio turned back to Leo: 'Don't–

Leo was already halfway out on the pitch.

'–overdo it!' he finished.

★ ★ ★

Leo, now on the pitch, shot Grandma Celia one of his big smiles. Then, in the next ten minutes, scored two goals and won the match for Newell's, just like that. On his second goal, his teammates surrounded him, hugged him, and lifted him into the air. And when Leo was higher than the rest of his teammates, he looked over at the stands and waved. His Grandma Celia was on her feet, waving her arms excitedly, and although there were a lot of folks in the stands that day, he could pick out her cheering from the rest and it made him feel warm and complete.

When his teammates lowered him back down to the field, he never saw her grab her stomach and cough. He had no idea she was not feeling well herself and she made sure no one else knew. Especially Leo. It would not do to have him see her sick, not when he had just scored the winning goal. She sat back down and took a deep breath and the pain finally faded away.

CHAPTER 9

GRANDMA

Leo threw his football bag over his shoulder and ran into the street as a flatbed truck ambled by. He always hitched a ride on some truck or other when he was late and needed to get to the pitch in a hurry. He caught up with it at the next corner, jumped on the back, lay back on the hard wood bed, and looked up at the pure azure sky.

When the truck slowed in front of Malvina's, Leo hopped off and waved thanks as it continued up the dirt road. Then he looked both ways and raced across the street, through the gate and into the Newell's Old Boys dressing room.

★ ★ ★

The pitch was still wet, but Leo did not care. He dropped his favourite ball on his foot and started juggling it, keeping it from hitting the ground, bouncing it from one knee to the other to the top of his head and back to his ankle where he scooped it up before it touched the grass and sent it back to his chest. He looked over at the stands and waved to his Grandma Celia. She was not there. He let the ball drop to the grass. He looked around, up and down the stands. Maybe she changed seats. He looked and looked, but could not find her.

He finally shrugged and charged down the pitch towards the opposing goal, dribbling the ball, warming up. Suddenly he heard a voice shouting at him from behind. 'Leo!' It was Cintia and she was running after him! What was she *doing,* he thought. Was she crazy? Whatever she was doing, she was starting to catch up to him, so he poured it on and ran full-throttle away from her, but when he looked back to see where she was, all he could see her was her face, streaked with tears. He stopped in the middle of the pitch and she ran up to him and said something in his ear.

Leo grabbed her hand and both of them rushed off the pitch, never stopping when they passed his teammates and his coaches and out into the street, turning left and heading straight home, leaving everyone at Newell's Old Boys befuddled and bewildered.

A few minutes later, Leo knew it was bad when he walked in the front door. There were many grown-ups in the living room, speaking quietly to his mother, who was sitting on the couch, sobbing, wiping her tears with a handkerchief. One would take her hand and kiss it and she would nod and wipe her eyes. When she saw Leo, she hid her eyes for a moment and when she lowered her handkerchief, she managed a small smile and stood up. Leo rushed over to her and she wrapped her arms around him and held him tight. 'She's gone, Leo,' his mother said. 'Grandma Celia has gone to heaven.'

Leo shoved his face into his mother's apron just as he did all those years growing up. He did not want anyone to see him cry. Grandma had been sick for a while, but never too ill to miss one of his

games. He felt pain. The most pain he had ever felt
in his life was when he was run over by a cyclist in
the street. This was worse. He closed his eyes and
saw his Grandma Celia's face, smiling upon him.
He remembered her giving him his first ball and all
the times she stuck up for him and how she talked
Coach Apa into putting him on the team and how
she personally talked the Newell's coaches into
trying him out. She was there for every important
moment of his life and now she was gone and Leo
did not know what to do. He did not know how
he could live the rest of his life without her. He hid
his face in his mother's apron and he felt his father
come over and wrap his arms around them both
and they all cried in the centre of the room. But not
Leo. He held back the tears.

He finally took a deep breath, then pulled away
from his mother and father and raced out of the
house. He did not stop running until he got to his
secret place in the hills. And there, alone in the
hills, he wept. Where no one but God could see
him. He prayed and he spoke to his Grandma Celia.

After a few minutes, Leo heard someone coming his way, and he wiped his face with his shirt. He could not let anyone see him crying like this. But it wasn't his mother or his father. It was Cintia. 'I knew you would be here,' she said softly.

Leo was relieved and leaned on her and she put her arm over his shoulders and held him up. 'I can't believe you came up here, Cintia,' he said.

'I've never seen you cry before,' she said, soothing him.

'Yeah, you have. When we were next to each other getting our diapers changed,' Leo said.

Cintia giggled, and then realized it was a sad occasion. 'Sorry,' she said, embarrassed.

'Grandma is in heaven now,' Leo said and crossed himself, then looked up into the azure sky over Rosario and raised two fingers up, one on each hand.

'What's that for?' Cintia asked.

'That's my next goal. For Grandma Celia,' Leo replied. 'I'm okay now. Let's go back.'

Cintia nodded, and together they hiked back down the hill to Leo's house.

When Leo stepped inside, there were family and friends and neighbours everywhere, but his mother and father were nowhere to be seen. He searched every room and finally found them sitting side-by-side on their bed. He came in and squeezed between them and leaned against his father. His mother was holding an open envelope from the Social Security Foundation.

'I grew another inch,' he said, trying to lighten the mood.

Leo's mother just started sobbing again. 'First mama and now this,' she said, waving the envelope.

'What is that?' Leo asked, fearing the worst.

Jorge took the envelope from his wife and turned to Leo. 'My work and – Social Security – they can no longer pay for your medicine,' Jorge hesitated.

'Don't bother the boy with this, Jorge,' Celia said softly, clasping Leo's hand in hers.

'You mean, I won't grow anymore?' Leo asked.

Leo's mum looked to her husband, then wiped her face with her apron. 'Absolutely not,' she said with stern resolve. 'It means your father and I will find another way to help pay our medical bills.' She turned to Jorge. 'Right?'

Jorge looked at his beautiful wife and took her face in his hands. 'Right.'

CHAPTER 10

THE QUEST

Leo, Matias, Rodrigo, and even little Maria Sol hid
in the bedroom, peeked out the doorway,
and listened to their parents talk loudly at the
dinner table. 'I'll go there alone, if I have to,'
Leo's father said.

'Do you really think if the Social Security
Foundation can't pay, that Newell's *will?*' Leo's
mother asked, full of doubt.

'I don't know, but I'm going to find out,' Leo's
father countered, taking her hand. 'I know one
thing. We can't give up now.'

Leo slumped against the bedroom wall,
surrounded by his brothers and little sister and

blew out a breath. There was a long, loud silence coming from the other room. His sweat ran down his forehead and burned his eyes. 'But it's not my fault!' he whispered to himself.

Matias smacked him lightly in the head. 'Knock it off. It's nobody's fault. Papa will fix this.'

The very next day, Jorge and Celia were seated across from a modest desk in the president's office of Newell's Old Boys. Celia was already halfway to tears and Jorge had his speech ready. When the Newell's president walked into the room, Jorge stood up and took a deep breath.

The president was medium height wearing a dark suit and tie to offset his thick salt-and-pepper beard. 'Mr and Mrs Messi, how nice of you to come. Please, Mr Messi,' the president said, waving his hand as if brushing him off. 'Sit, sit.'

Jorge stuck out his hand and the president grasped it and shook it, noticing Jorge still had not sat down. The president waited, then finally said, 'Sit, Mr Messi. I know why you are here.'

'You do?' Jorge asked, slowly lowering himself

into his chair. He was not sure if he liked this guy. They had barely had any contact with him the whole time Leo was playing for Newell's Old Boys. He certainly was not anything like the man who was president when *he* was a boy on the team.

As soon as Jorge sat down, the president did the same. 'Of course I do. I know everything about our boys. For instance, I know that Leo's medical bills are more than you can handle and that your employer has stopped paying,' he said.

'I'm surprised you know such personal things about us,' Jorge said.

'Don't be,' the man said. 'It is my job to know. Newell's pays me to make sure everyone in our great club is… happy. Not only the players, but the families of the players as well.'

Celia gripped Jorge's hand tightly.

'We think Leo has great potential,' the man said.

The president got up and sat on the corner of his desk. 'And we want to help.'

Jorge pushed back in his chair and let out a

breath of relief. Celia took his hand and squeezed
so tight he grimaced in pain.

The president stood up and so did Celia and
Jorge. 'If you can figure out a way to pay half of
Leo's medical expenses, Newell's Old Boys will pay
the other half.'

The joy of the moment was cut in half and faded
away.

'Half,' Celia said, doing the maths in her head.
That would be at least $500 per month. They
are offering to pay for every other injection, she
thought.

Before she could speak, Jorge blurted out: 'We'll
take it, sir.'

They shook hands and the president promised he
would be in touch with the details but to expect a
cheque soon. Celia was humble and thanked the
man profusely.

The first time the Newell's cheque was late,
neither Celia nor Jorge thought much of it. But
after a time, the cheque came later and later and
finally stopped coming altogether. And they were

right back where they started with no way to pay for Leo's large medical bills. Another crisis was looming.

★ ★ ★

One more time, Jorge and Celia faced each other across the dinner table. Leo and the rest of the kids peeked in from the bedroom door and listened as their parents came to a decision. If Newell's Old Boys would not help Leo with his medical bills, they would find a team that would. Jorge and Celia vowed not to stop until they exhausted every possibility. Jorge knew in his heart that Leo could be a professional player, so there was only one place left: the best team in all of Argentina. That night Celia packed Jorge's and Leo's backpacks. The next morning, they were heading to Buenos Aires.

CHAPTER 11

CLUB ATLÉTICO RIVER PLATE

The bus to Buenos Aires was five minutes late. Leo and his father stood at the corner down the street from their house, waiting. They were dressed up for the trip. The stiff collar on Leo's shirt bothered him and he squirmed in it. He could not wait to pull it off and put on a jersey. Jorge wore slacks and a white shirt and tie and constantly pulled at the collar because it was too tight.

The bus ride to Buenos Aires was four hours long. The vinyl seats were torn and repaired with orange, gray, and yellow tape and Leo's legs kept sticking to it. The bus was old and his window was stuck halfway down. And no matter how hard he tried, he could not close it. For a couple of hours, both he and his father choked back the fumes from the traffic on the highway until finally, Jorge had had enough and shoved his sport coat into the half-open window.

★ ★ ★

Buenos Aires, shrouded in mist, appeared out of nowhere when the bus arrived at the station on Avenida Presidente Figueroa Alcorta. Leo and Jorge were just a few short blocks from River Plate Stadium, the biggest football facility in the city. The stadium rested on a short hill overlooking the city and looked like a stack of mama's dinner bowls. They would take a taxi from the bus station to the stadium.

Leo bounced on his seat in the back of the taxi and pressed his nose against the glass as the stadium whisked past. 'Aren't we stopping?' he asked.

'The tryout pitch is just another block,' the taxi driver said.

Leo sat back in his seat, disappointed. He had hoped to play in the great stadium where Club Atlético River Plate icons Gabriel Batistuta and Hernán Crespo scored many beautiful goals. Jorge recognized the look on his son's face and punched his shoulder. 'You'll get to the stadium soon enough, Leo,' he said.

'You guys fans?' the cab driver said.

Both Leo and his father looked at each other. 'We are from Rosario,' Jorge said.

'Ah! *Lepers* fans!' the driver laughed. 'You must be miserable.'

'I never complain about my family to strangers,' Jorge said, and he and the taxi driver shared a laugh.

★ ★ ★

The training grounds near River Plate Stadium were the best Leo had ever seen. The grass was green and perfectly manicured, the lines were undamaged, and the goal nets were perfect, not covered in multi-coloured threads from mothers of team members sewing up holes. Leo was excited as he walked through the gates and on to the pitch. The first thing he saw was that all the boys who were trying out for the youth team were lined up. He joined the end of the line and waited patiently.

Jorge wanted to get closer to his son, but he had to stay on the other side of the chain-link fence. When he saw Leo take his place at the end of the line, he pressed his face against the fence. The coaches ignored Leo and Jorge did not want him left out. He waved his arms and pointed to Leo.

Out on the centreline, on the other side of the fence, Leo saw his father jumping around like a wild man and pointing at him. He looked away, embarrassed, but secretly smiled to himself.

The tryout was in full swing. Each player had a big paper number clipped to his jersey. Two teams were formed: the Yellow Team versus the Red Team. There were maybe seventy kids waiting to be called in. The coaches closely followed the players around, taking notes. Each player got five minutes to prove themselves. The best players got ten. That was it. Leo waited patiently, hoping they would not forget him. He was tired of waiting, but hungry to get out there and touch the ball.

Finally, one of the coaches pointed at him and a bunch of other kids and told them to get in.

Jorge yelled from the other side of the fence. He wanted Leo to get close to the pack that was attacking the ball. Leo seemed lost at first. Then he looked at his father. A second later, he darted and charged at an incredible pace. He stole the ball from a player on the other team and rocketed toward the goal. He passed a number of players and then shot a curved ball with his left foot that went straight past the diving keeper and into the net!

Jorge let out a sigh of relief.

★ ★ ★

The River Plate coaches watched Leo's whole performance. They let him stay on the pitch another ten minutes and in those minutes, Leo scored two more goals and assisted another.

When they finally asked him to go out, the coach smiled at him. Leo sat on the sidelines with all the other kids. When the tryout was over, they called in five kids. Leo was one of them.

'Are your parents here?' one of the coaches asked softly.

'My father is over there,' Leo said, pointing to Jorge.

The coach nodded and the two men walked towards each other and shook hands. 'We want him,' the coach said. 'Bring him to River Plate.' Then he walked away and turned his attention to the remaining boys.

★ ★ ★

Jorge's heart thumped in his chest. Leo did it. He had passed the test in front of one of the greatest teams in Argentina.

'What did he say?' Leo asked.

'They want you here, son,' said his father, trying to hide his excitement.

Leo smiled. He knew he had played well and he

thought they liked him, but he did not want to brag.

'Did you tell him I play for Newell's Old Boys?' Leo asked innocently.

Jorge's mood changed immediately. Leo noticed the change and looked up at his father. 'What's wrong?'

Jorge never mentioned the *Lepers* to the River Plate coaches when he signed his son up. And Newell's would not let Leo go without a fight… or a price. Jorge looked around the pitch, trying to find the coach and finally spotted him near the gate, watching the other players. 'Wait here, Leo,' Jorge said, and trotted over to the coach.

'Sir, I need you to know, my son Leo plays for Newell's Old Boys and,' Jorge hesitated.

The coach was not happy to hear the news. 'Newell's?! Does he have a contract?'

Jorge pursed his lips. 'Yes,' he said. 'Yes, he does.'

'Well, you see, now we have a problem,' the coach said and got in Jorge's face. 'We will have to negotiate for him,' he said, exasperated. 'And those clubs always want a lot of money.'

'Well, I'm sure that you can come to some sort of an agree–'

The coach cut him off. 'Forget it.' He gave Jorge a cursory nod. 'Good day. Thank you for showing him to us but we are not interested.' He turned on his heel and walked away without another word.

Jorge watched helplessly as the coach walked out of their lives and saw Leo's last chance at medical treatments walk away with him. After a moment, Jorge composed himself and turned to Leo, who rushed up to him. 'What did he say, Papa?'

Jorge did not know what to say to his son. He closed his eyes and asked for the words to tell his son. 'You are not going to play for River Plate, son,' Jorge finally said to him. 'There are greater things in store for you.'

'But I thought I played great today,' Leo said, fighting back tears, not knowing what to say or do. He suddenly felt empty and wished his Grandma Celia was here. She would know what to do.

'It's not about how you played, Leo. It's about

the business of football. You were great out there. But there is all this money involved,' Jorge soothed his son.

'What should we do?' Leo asked.

'Leave it to me. I will take care of this. You just play and do not worry. Things will come our way,' Jorge said. 'They have to.' He searched for the words, then added: 'You see? They wanted you! That is the key. You passed the test. If River Plate saw what you have to offer, so will others.' Jorge felt better. His own words calmed him. He smiled at his son.

Leo thought about it for a long time. His father's confidence was comforting. 'I felt good out there,' he said. 'But I know I can be even better.'

'Good,' Jorge said draping his arm around his son's shoulders and guiding him towards the gate. 'That's called "perseverance". You're well on your way. Let's go home.'

And as Jorge and Leo walked off the Club Atlético River Plate pitch, they never saw the man in the stands suddenly get up, rush out to the street, and fly into a nearby phone booth where he nervously fumbled money into the slot and made a long distance call.

CHAPTER 12

THE STRANGER

'What are we going to do?' Celia asked Jorge, pouring him a steaming hot cup of coffee. The kitchen table, usually filled with food and family, was empty except for them. The bus ride back from Buenos Aires was four hours of restless sleep and regret.

Although Jorge knew how good Leo was, he realized for the time being, there was no team in Argentina who wanted his son badly enough. He needed another solution, but from where?

There was a knock at the door.

'Are you expecting company?' Celia asked.

'No,' Jorge said, standing.

Leo heard the knock first, rushed to the front door, and yanked it open. A tall man he had never seen before stood on the porch looking down at him with a stern face, but kind eyes. He was well dressed in a suit. Leo immediately knew this was a stranger from somewhere else because he was not used to the Rosario heat.

'Are you Leo?' the stranger asked and smiled. 'I came a long way to see you.'

The stranger introduced himself and offered his hand. 'My name is Juan Gaspar,' he said. 'And I've come all the way from Barcelona to speak with you and your parents.'

'Barcelona?' Jorge said, astonished, shaking his hand and started to realize this was no ordinary stranger.

'Yes, I represent FC Barcelona,' Gaspar replied.

'B-Barça?' Leo stammered.

Gaspar smiled and nodded. 'Yes, Leo, Barça,' Gaspar said. 'Perhaps you have heard of us?' he kidded.

Even Leo knew he was joking. Everyone in Rosario had heard of Barça.

'Come in Mr Gaspar,' Celia offered. 'Would you like something cold to drink? Water? Lemonade?'

Mr Gaspar nodded and entered the room and sat near the table.

Gaspar drank homemade lemonade and then had coffee and Leo's favourite biscuits, Alfajores. Over bites of food, he explained how some men in Buenos Aires had seen Leo and phoned Horacio Gaggioli, an agent for FC Barcelona. Gaggioli had gone directly to Joseph Maria Minguella, who had coached the Barcelona youth team and brought many football stars to Barça. Because Gaspar's job was scouting new talent for the club, Minguella sent him across the Atlantic to Rosario to see a boy who was knocking everyone's socks off. It was the first time in club history that Barça sent a scout to look for talent in a country other than Spain.

'We're making history here,' Mr Gaspar said, munching another sweet Alfajore, smiling.

The Messis had relatives in the mountainous city of Lerida, which was about seventy-five miles from Barcelona. Because of this, everyone at Barça thought Spain would have no problem accepting Leo as one of their own.

Celia thought everything was moving too quickly. 'Leo is too young to move to Barcelona,' Celia said.

Mr Gaspar soothed her nerves by telling them all about the Barcelona FC academy, La Masia. It was a big old farmhouse opposite Camp Nou, the Barcelona stadium where kids from all over Spain were schooled in all academic subjects. And in their spare time, they were schooled in the game of football by the great coaching staff of FC Barcelona. 'They get the best education and the best football education all in one,' explained their guest. 'They learn values and manners and we also teach them how to be great in their future profession as football players.'

'Well, we wouldn't all be able to go and the family has never split up before,' Celia said, talking to Jorge and the kids. Maria Sol was in her high chair getting food all over her, ignoring the discussion.

'It was Grandma Celia's dream,' Leo said.

The room grew pin-drop quiet. Gaspar looked at him intently. 'There is one more thing,' he said, saving the best for last. 'If Leo is accepted to La Masia, we will pay all his medical bills.'

The entire living room grew suddenly silent. Everyone stopped breathing.

'What do you think, Mr Messi?' Gaspar asked after a moment.

Jorge smiled. 'Who am I to question a miracle?'

Mr Gaspar flashed a smile.

'But even if we move to Barcelona,' Jorge continued. 'Where would I work? I need to support my family.'

Gaspar nodded. He expected these questions. 'The club will help you find a job. Barça will make things happen, Mr Messi,' he said, smiling again.

★ ★ ★

Half an hour later, Gaspar sat on the living room sofa, a phone cradled in his ear.

Jose Maria Minguella picked up on the first

ring. It was morning in Barcelona and he had been expecting the call from his scout. He said his pleasantries, and then made a conference call through to the Barça coach, Charly Rexach, who was in Australia for the Olympics. The three men on three different continents were now talking about a kid from Rosario, Argentina. It was the middle of the night for Charly Rexach and unlike Minguella; he would have preferred to be sleeping. 'How old is he?' Rexach asked groggily.

'Twelve,' Gaspar said.

'You know, I specifically asked for an eighteen-year-old,' Rexach said.

'Leo Messi plays better than an eighteen-year-old,' Gaspar quickly shot back.

'Is this true, Señor Minguella?'

'Looking at the tapes, the boy is exceptional,' Minguella came back immediately.

Rexach sighed on the other end as the first rays of the sun peeked up over the horizon outside his window. 'I'll meet you and the boy in Barcelona in two weeks,' he said.

'Thank you!' Gaspar said loudly. He was excited and quickly said goodbye to Minguella who had to get off and head to work.

'You better be right, Gaspar,' Rexach said and hung up.

Gaspar smiled to himself, gently placed the phone in its cradle and triumphantly whispered to himself, 'I am.'

CHAPTER 13

LOSING SIGHT OF THE SHORE

Leo pressed his nose against the window and watched the Argentine landscape drift by below them and thought it looked like a chequerboard.

Secretly, he did not like being too far away from his Rosario home, so this trip was a big deal. Losing sight of the shore made him nervous. He tried to relax as he stretched out in his seat and smiled as it squeaked under him.

The flight to Barcelona, Spain, took fifteen hours. Leo tried watching the movies but all he could think about was playing for Barça. He looked at his father. Sound asleep. He shrugged and got up and went to the front flight station on the aircraft where several flight attendants were busy packing away dishes. 'Remember when you said if there was anything I wanted, I should just ask?'

'Of course,' said one of the attendants. 'What can we do for you?'

'I want to watch *Baby's Day Out*,' Leo said. 'It's a movie.'

The attendants looked at each other. The steward was amused. 'I would have guessed *Die Hard* maybe, but not *Baby's Day Out*.

'It's my favourite movie,' Leo said. 'It's about a baby who escapes from home and goes on lots of adventures in the big city. No one expects the baby to do amazing things.'

'Especially the baby,' a flight attendant said and everyone shared a laugh.

★ ★ ★

Fifteen hours later, Leo and his father rode in a taxi from the airport to their hotel. The drive took them right through the heart of Barcelona and straight to their hotel, which was near the Camp

Nou Stadium. Leo kept his face pressed against the window for the entire twenty-minute drive and marvelled at the Barcelona skyline. He had never seen a city like this before.

Two days later, Leo could not stand being cooped up anymore. For two days, Leo and his father stayed in the hotel and came down the elevator eight floors only to eat and to check for messages. But none came. Knowing that Camp Nou was only up the street from where they were staying drove Leo crazy. He had to see it, but Jorge said they needed to stay close to the room in case the team called.

When he could not take the waiting anymore, Leo grabbed his ball, snuck out of his room, and raced down the hallway to the elevators.

CHAPTER 14

THE END OF THE RAINBOW

When the elevator reached the lobby and the
doors whispered open, Leo peered out, first in one
direction, then the other. The coast was clear. He
trotted to the front door of the hotel and it opened
automatically for him. In two more seconds, he
was out of the hotel and on to Avenida Sabino
de Arana. Although it was quiet in the hotel, the
street was a symphony of cars and trucks, buses
and motorbikes; steady streams of traffic in both
directions right in front of him. Leo looked right
and there in the distance was Camp Nou Stadium:
the biggest, highest coliseum he had ever seen.
He dropped his ball, gave it a kick, and charged

up the pavement after it, shifting it from one foot to the other as he ran as fast as he could, faking around pedestrians, bouncing it off the trees that lined the busy street, always in total control.

When Leo reached Camp Nou, all the gates were locked. He expected this. He looked ahead and there was the Museum Store. Tourists were going inside to buy souvenirs and look at the pitch through the windows. He stopped and pulled a folded piece of paper from his back pocket. It was a map of the stadium. He studied it intently then refolded it and shoved it back in his pocket. He was almost there. He charged off, kicking the ball along with him and weaved through the tourists going into the Museum Store. Around the next bend, with the store out of sight, he stopped. This was what he was looking for: one of the service gates. Just like in the picture, he thought. He waited. And waited. Ten minutes passed. Then he heard it: the faint whine of an electric engine. It grew closer and closer and finally the service gate swung open and a man on a service cart loaded with boxes drove through and headed back towards the Museum Store. Leo was pressed against the fence and when the cart turned left, he spun left. The gates closed automatically. Leo was inside!

He stopped in his tracks. There it was, right in front of him. The Camp Nou pitch. The stands were massive and reached up into the sky. They were now empty except for a few custodians sweeping the rows. To Leo, they looked like ants. He had dreamed of being here his entire life and now he was staring out onto one of the world's greatest football pitches. He picked up his ball and respectfully and cautiously entered the stadium. He approached the sideline closest to him but did not dare cross it. Playing here at Camp Nou is an *earned* honour, he thought. He still had not received a contract from Barça, so there was no way he was going to kick the ball around here. Besides, he was not here to see the pitch. He had something else in mind.

He knew where to go. He did not even have to look at the map. He walked around the pitch, entered the tunnel on the other side, and when he emerged from the tunnel, he stopped.

Just in front of him was another football pitch, this one considerably smaller than the stadium pitch. It was nestled between Avinguda de Joan XXIII and Carrer De La Maternitat roads and beyond this mini pitch was what he was looking for. He recognized the old building immediately. 'La Masia!' he muttered to himself as he stepped closer.

Leo knew everything there was to know about La Masia. For instance he knew that it was built in 1702 as housing for the architects who built Camp Nou when it was a military camp. He knew that when Camp Nou became the home of FC Barcelona, La Masia became the residence hall of the youth team players. Leo knew everything about La Masia except for one thing. He had no idea what it was like on the inside.

Leo stepped towards the big wooden doors of La Masia as they suddenly opened and a young player about his age appeared on the doorstep and was instantly joined by two more players a little older than him.

Leo stopped and froze. He wanted to run. But before he could, the first player glared at him threateningly and said: 'What are you doing here?'

Leo replied nervously in his own Spanish dialect that he had come in through the service gate from the road. He used the Argentine word, *portrero,* which sounded a lot like the Catalan word for goalie, *porter.* The boys burst out laughing. 'You came in from the goalie?' They laughed some more and moved towards him. 'I think we're going to have to toss you out,' the tall one on the left said.

Leo didn't wait for him to finish his sentence. He spun and raced down the short hill. The three boys watched him run and laughed. The one called Xavi turned to the third boy, the one about Leo's age, and said: 'Let's go back inside and finish our lunch, Cesc.' The boys nodded in agreement and went back into La Masia.

Leo didn't stop running until he sprinted up to the service gate and stomped on the sensor in the asphalt. When the gate opened automatically, he raced through, and once more found himself on the Avenida Sabino de Arana, and did not stop until he had returned to his hotel up the street.

★ ★ ★

Jorge sat in a chair, mesmerized, as Leo spun the tale of his adventures that day. He made his son tell him every detail down to the height of the boys and the colours of their jerseys. Leo stood in the middle of the room and described the boys and Jorge just shook his head in wonderment. 'What an amazing day you had!' Jorge said, hugging his son tight to him. 'Too bad you didn't get a look at the inside of La Masia!'

'Some day, Papa,' Leo said. 'Some day.'

CHAPTER 15

THE WAIT

Jorge angrily threw his clothes into his suitcase. 'I can't believe these guys,' he said, tossing his last pair of pants into the bag and slamming the lid, sitting on it to squish it down, then zipping it up.

Leo was on the other side of the room, sadly taking his clothes from a drawer, one by one, and dropping them into his open suitcase on the bed. 'Why haven't they made a deal?' Jorge said, coming over to his son to help him pack. 'Two weeks!' he said. 'No one should have to wait two weeks for anything!' He snatched up a pair of Leo's underwear, looked at it, and grimaced, then dropped it into his bag. 'Do you ever *wash* these things?'

Leo sighed and nodded.

Jorge had spoken to someone from FC Barcelona almost every day, mostly the scout, Gaspar. And every day he promised that tomorrow, the head trainer, Señor Rexach, would return from the Olympics in Australia and watch Leo play. Jorge was convinced his son would surely be accepted to the FC Barcelona Youth Team and Barça would make a deal with them. Nevertheless, the days passed, Rexach did not come, and Jorge's patience flew out the window. To Jorge, it looked as if they were going home empty-handed.

Whenever Jorge was nervous, Leo was nervous. It was a father-son thing. Leo was sad to see his father this way and was worried he would never get over it. For Leo, the most important thing was to play the game. If he could not do it here, he would do it back home. Leo's bag was finally packed and Jorge picked up the telephone and dialed a number. When Gaspar answered, he told him they were packed and ready to return to Rosario.

Gaspar was desperate. 'I beg of you, Mr Messi,'

Gaspar said into the phone at the other end. 'Stay for one more day. We have arranged for a little game tomorrow with some of the older boys. Mr Rexach has returned from the Olympics and he has promised to come see Leo play. What do you say? One more day?'

Jorge put the receiver to his chest and looked across the room at his son, who sat on his suitcase, trying to squish it down far enough to lock it. Leo looked over with pleading eyes. Jorge sighed. 'All right, Señor Gaspar. One more day.'

Leo flashed the biggest smile Jorge had ever seen. Jorge calmly hung up the phone and Leo ran into his arms. 'Thank you, Papa,' he said and nuzzled his face into his father's chest.

'No reason to thank me. Do you really believe I would let this grand opportunity pass you by? Like they say,' Jorge said, 'Sometimes you have to play tough.'

Leo hugged him tighter.

Leo beamed. Although he had been waiting for two weeks, he could not wait until tomorrow.

★ ★ ★

The next morning Leo ran all the way to Camp Nou. Today was the day, he thought. Today was the day he would join the youth team. They would be watching him. He needed to bring his best to today's exhibition game. You never knew who was watching. His father walked at a more leisurely pace and enjoyed the sights along Sabino de Arana, proud of himself for putting his foot down with FC Barcelona. The scheduled game with the fourteen-year-olds at Camp Number 3 in the *Miniestadi,* the smaller stadium adjacent to the main Camp Nou Stadium, would start punctually at 1pm.

When Leo arrived near the locker room, the team was already lined up on a small expanse of grass. The coach spotted him immediately and called him over: 'Leo! Over here!' he said.

Leo marched up and found a place in the line-up. The boys who had scared Leo the other day at the front door of La Masia, Andrés Iniesta, Xavi, and Cesc Fabregas, were already in line.

'Everyone, I want you to meet our new forward, Leo Messi!' the coach, said, draping his arm over Leo's shoulders. The entire team applauded him. Leo could not believe it.

'La Masia is for those who earn it!' Xavi said and all three boys chuckled.

Leo, embarrassed, nodded as the trio slapped his back.

The coach ran by, urging the boys to get ready. 'You're up front, Leo,' he said as he rushed past.

Minutes later, out on the pitch, Leo happily took his forward position.

He looked left and Cesc winked at him, flashing a big smile. He looked back and there was Andrés taking up the left midfield with Xavi right behind him, manning the centre of midfield.

Leo stood planted in the grass for that split second, surrounded by Xavi, Andrés, and Cesc, and knew he could do anything. The wait was over.

The game started.

They were playing against the under-14 youth squad, and those guys were tough. From the first pass, Leo felt fantastic. He knew the guys would trust him once they saw him in action. It was always like that. And when he earned their trust, they would pass him the ball and he would do what he always did, make that final pass for an assist or finish off a beautiful run with a goal. He knew everything would fall into place. It was the most important game of his life. But he felt calm. At ease. No matter where he was, once he stepped onto the pitch, it was his world. His home.

Leo knew the Barça system of Tika-Taka after watching so many matches on TV. He had taught it to himself all the way back in Rosario. Short passes in rhythm. Receive. Pass. Move.

And then it happened. He got the ball from Andrés and made the run into the box with the ball glued to his left foot. Time stood still. The defenders could not keep up with him. They were U14 Barca players and he was two years younger and a foot shorter, but it didn't really matter. Leo was a bolt of lightning, and the ball flew high into the net.

Leo's first goal in the Barça world.

Everyone in the stands was on their feet, cheering wildly. The roar of the crowd beat against Leo's chest and inspired him. He raised his fingers to the heavens and dedicated the goal to his Grandma Celia.

Carlos Rexach, the Technical Director of FC Barcelona arrived late, tired and jet-lagged from the flight from Australia. He entered Camp Number 3 as he always did, from the back, and walked the length of the field to his seat. Then he spotted Leo on the pitch. How could he miss him? He was the smallest kid out there. What was he doing with that ball? He fooled the opposition completely by shifting the ball from one foot to the other. Then, suddenly Leo stopped on a dime, shifted his weight, and turned around a full 180 degrees, and without hesitation, pushed the ball forward, always in control. A perfect change of direction. How could anyone that young and that small even *think* that way? He watched Leo intently in amazement.

Gaspar saw Rexach make his way down the

length of the pitch and was shocked when he saw the man stop and watch. Gaspar leapt over the railing and ran to Rexach and greeted him.

'Your seat is down here, sir,' Gaspar said with a twinkle in his eye.

Rexach chuckled. The scout knew him well. 'So this is our boy?' he asked.

'Leo Messi, sir,' Gaspar said proudly. 'The boy from Rosario. The one you came to see.'

'Thank you!' Rexach said, never taking his eyes off Leo.

Fifteen minutes later, after Leo scored two more goals, Rexach was on his feet cheering with the rest of the crowd. He turned excitedly to Gaspar and said: 'We have to sign him.'

'I think so too, sir,' Gaspar said, trying to hide his glee.

'This boy is different,' Rexach said. Leo reminded him of another genius from Argentina, one who helped Barça take the *double* in 1983, winning both the Copa del Rey and the Spanish Super Cup: Diego Maradona.

'I'd better tell you, his father was quite angry with us, making them wait two weeks. I had to calm him down and talk him into staying. They had their bags packed and were ready to leave.'

Rexach looked at Gaspar and nodded. The boy was a prodigy to be sure. He could not let him out of his grasp. He would never forgive himself. 'Well, Gaspar, my friend,' Rexach said, draping his arm over Gaspar's shoulders. 'If Leo Messi can wait fifteen days for me to arrive, then I can make a decision about him in one day.'

'Yes, sir,' Gaspar said, happily.

Rexach shook his head in wonderment as Leo continued to dominate against the older team.

'Let's talk to his father,' he said.

CHAPTER 16

THE NAPKIN

Leo stood in the middle of the Barcelona Airport
terminal with his father and when he saw his
mother and Maria Sol come off the plane, he ran
into his mother's arms and hugged her tight. Celia
Messi sobbed, overwhelmed by the welcome, and
Leo could feel her shudder and squeezed her even
tighter. Tears streaked his face and he did not care.
He stopped hiding his tears when his Grandma
Celia died. Jorge joined in the hug as Celia Messi
pulled a handkerchief from her purse and wiped her
own tears then handed it to Leo and he laughed. He
had missed her so much and now she was finally
here. He had not seen her in a month.

Matias and Rodrigo came off next and when they saw their little brother, they slammed into him and almost knocked him over. 'The Three Musketeers!' Matias shouted. 'Back together again!' He shoved his hand into Leo's hair and messed it up. Then Jorge moved in and the entire Messi family shared a group hug, with Leo in the middle, right in the middle of the Barcelona Airport terminal. When they finished hugging, they all walked out of the terminal together. 'Does he have a contract?' Celia asked Jorge as they walked.

'Not exactly,' Jorge said, hesitantly. FC Barcelona had been paying for everything, but Leo still did not have a written contract.

'"Not exactly" is not a "yes",' Celia said, shooting her husband a look.

'They say it's coming,' Jorge said, holding the door for his wife.

She looked up at him. She knew he was doing everything possible to help their son. They had come a long way this time after being rejected a couple of times already. This was the furthest they had ever come and she was nervous it might fall apart at the last second, just as it did at Newell's and at River Plate. Instead of criticizing Jorge, she kissed her husband on the cheek and told him he was doing a great job and they all moved towards the car that was waiting to take them back to the hotel. Jorge climbed into the car last and put his arm around Celia's shoulders. It was a long flight and she was happy to have the whole family back together again. 'Rexach says it will be any day now,' he whispered in her ear.

★ ★ ★

'Two months!' Celia said, turning from the window overlooking the city of Barcelona. Jorge could see the frustration in her face. It had been almost two months since they had stepped off the plane from Rosario. Still there was no contract. She decided she had to put her foot down. 'Barcelona is beginning to look a lot like Newell's and River Plate and Leo needs his injections. We are running out of money. We risked everything and all we have to show for it is this hotel room and a pile of dirty laundry. If they are not going to give Leo a contract, we should go home.'

Matias and Rodrigo watched TV in the bedroom but Leo had his ear pressed against the closed door and listened to his mother and father intently.

'Okay, I'll make the call,' Jorge said. 'I'll call Charly Rexach.'

★ ★ ★

The boardroom of FC Barcelona was elegant. A long antique table dominated the room. One wall was made entirely of glass and overlooked the Camp Nou Stadium. When Charly Rexach came in, the other managers, scouts, agents, and executives were already there.

'Remind us again, Charly,' said Joseph Maria Minguella before Rexach could even take his seat. Minguella was the head of FC Barcelona. 'Why are we being asked to hire a thirteen-year-old boy from Rosario, Argentina?'

'Because you asked me to find you the best,'

Rexach said, grinning, taking his seat. The rest of the members at the table laughed. 'And how would it look on my CV if I didn't deliver to you, not just the best youngster we've seen, but perhaps the best investment this club would make in years?'

Minguella smiled at his old friend Charly Rexach. 'I would expect nothing less.'

'The boy is obviously very special, sir.' Horacio Gaggioli the agent, chimed in. 'You asked us to look for talent outside of Spain and we found you the best.'

Minguella looked from one member of his team to the other.

'He is too young,' argued one of the managers.

'And too small,' said another.

'And that is what makes him all the more amazing,' said Gaggioli.

'I was twelve when I joined Barça,' Rexach said, locking eyes with him.

There was a long, loud silence in the room.

'Times are tough for our youth team,' said Minguella. 'You must know that, Charly.'

'And our job is to invest in the club's future. Why else did we send Gaspar on his grand quest to Argentina?' said Rexach.

'Messi is exactly what we need,' Gaspar said.

Rexach got up and walked down the table to where Minguella sat and stopped in front of him. 'Sir, I asked them for an eighteen-year-old. When Gaspar brought me a thirteen-year-old, I was angry. And then I watched the boy play.' Rexach shook his head in wonderment. 'He is different. And we can make him great!'

It took Joseph Maria Minguella a long time to answer. 'You better be right, Charly,' he finally said. 'We have a lot riding on him.'

'Yeah,' Rexach said. 'But so does his family. They risked it all to come here. I want permission to offer him a contract.' With that, he turned on his heel and returned to his seat.

When Rexach had settled in his chair, Joseph Maria Minguella smiled at him and nodded. 'Permission granted, Charly. We'll have something drawn up. It might take a while.'

Rexach stood up. 'With all due respect, sir, we don't have a while.'

Minguella studied his friend and knew he was serious. But there were channels they had to go through. The Barça machine was not something a kid from Rosario was going to change.

Charly Rexach took the elevator down to the street, knowing what he had to do. He walked to the nearest phone booth, called Jorge Messi and invited him and his son Leo to lunch. The Christmas decorations were already up all over the city and they made him happy as he strolled to the Pompeia Tennis Club. It was going to be a Merry Christmas for the Messi family.

Jorge and Leo were already at a table at the club when Rexach showed up. Most everyone in the restaurant knew him, so he spent a few lingering moments greeting friends and acquaintances, working his way through the crowded room to Jorge and Leo's table where they were drinking limeade and munching buscuits. Although the air was still warm, it was already the 14th of December.

Jorge was ready for Rexach when he pulled alongside their table and sat down. 'Did you bring the agreement?' Jorge asked anxiously.

Rexach shifted uncomfortably. 'Not yet,' he said. 'I need more time. You do not need to worry, I have been given permission to offer you a deal, but this is a big club and sometimes these things take time.'

Jorge was on the verge of exploding. 'Look, Leo needs his medical costs paid for and we are running out of money waiting for you. I hope you understand we have risked everything coming here. We cannot wait any longer. Either we get a contract or we go home.' Jorge was direct and to the point and Rexach liked that about him. He knew what he had to do.

'I couldn't agree more, Mr Messi. You want what is best for Leo, and so do we,' Rexach said, reaching into his suit coat, fishing out a pen. He patted himself down for something else, did not find it, so he stood up. 'Excuse me.' He crossed to the bar, snatched up a few napkins, hurried back to the table, unfolded one of the napkins on the table, and began writing. 'I believe you will be happy with the terms. Leo will live at La Masia and be fully paid. We will pick up all of his medical expenses, and we will find a job in the FC Barcelona organization for you, as well. Of course, you will have to agree to move to Spain and Leo will have to become a citizen, but that shouldn't be difficult since you have relatives in Lerida.' Rexach said, looking up from the cocktail napkin he had been scribbling on.

'A contract on a cocktail napkin!' Jorge said, amazed.

Leo laughed even though he was not sure exactly what the adults were talking about.

Rexach laughed too. 'I usually carry paper with me, but I was in a rush to see you.' He shoved the unfolded, scribbled-on napkin contract at Jorge. 'Tell me if I have I missed anything.'

Jorge eagerly looked over the improvised napkin contract, occasionally glancing at Leo and smiling. It was everything they had ever dreamed of and more. When he finished reading, he looked up at

Rexach and smiled, happier than he had ever been. He pushed the napkin back to the man from FC Barcelona and nodded. 'We have a deal.'

Charly Rexach breathed a sigh of relief. There were some people around the world, including those at Newell's Old Boys and River Plate in Argentina, who were going to regret they let this genius slip through their fingers.

When their lunch was over, Rexach thanked Jorge and Leo and promised to deliver a more formal contract as soon as he could deliver the napkin to Minguella and Gaggioli at FC Barcelona. When he unfolded it in front of Joseph Maria Minguella, the man who ran Barça laughed uproariously.

'A NAPKIN?!' Minguella shouted it so loudly that his secretary ran into the room with a handful of napkins for him, thinking he needed one. 'Right here, Señor Minguella!' she said, dangling a napkin in front of his face.

Minguella and Gaggioli and Rexach burst out laughing and their joy echoed through the halls of FC Barcelona.

CHAPTER 17

GOODBYE, THREE MUSKETEERS

Leo nervously stood once more in front of the grand doors of La Masia and knocked. This time the doors were opened for him. Cesc, Xavi, and Andrés were all there waiting *for him.* 'Welcome to your new home, Leo,' Cesc said.

Leo grinned. It was like he was living a dream.

A moment later he was in the place of his childhood dreams. The boys gave him the grand tour: they walked every hall in the place, peered into dorm rooms, and lingered in the kitchen, breathing in the aromas of the food prepared by the cooking staff. Their last stop was the computer room. And when the tour was over, Cesc, Xavi, and Andrés walked Leo back to the computer room. 'Welcome to your new football family,' Cesc said.

Leo beamed.

'Let's play football,' Cesc said.

'Now?!' Leo asked.

Cesc burst out laughing. 'FIFA!'

'On the big screen!' Andrés shouted.

They all went into the media room.

'I'm playing with Barça,' Cesc said.

'Then I'm playing with Old Boys,' said Leo.

'If I were you,' Cesc playfully warned Leo. 'I'd choose Arsenal. They are great!' he said.

★ ★ ★

Six weeks later, a messenger delivered a formal contract to Jorge and Leo Messi at their hotel, never realizing what he had just carried in his leather pouch.

Jorge Messi read over the contract from FC Barcelona and knew it was a fantastic deal for all of them. They would never have to worry about money again. But they always decided things as a family and this time was no exception.

'We do not need to *all* stay in Barcelona, Jorge,' Celia said. 'This is for you and Leo. The boys and Maria Sol need their home.'

'I miss my friends, Papa,' Matias said and his brother Rodrigo nodded in agreement.

'I miss Rosario too, Mama, but I have to play,' Leo said, hugging her. 'I have made new friends here.'

Jorge embraced his wife. 'I can't bear being without you,' he said softly.

'We'll talk every day,' she said. 'Make us proud, Leo,' Celia said. 'Grandma Celia will be smiling down on you from heaven.'

Jorge, Celia, Matias and Rodrigo surrounded Leo and one more time he was in the middle of a group hug. Even though his dreams were about to come true, he was scared.

Leo pulled away from his family and stared out of the big window at the city of Barcelona below. 'Papa, what if I'm not the *Pibe*,' he said.

'If you weren't,' his father said. 'We would not be here.'

'Remember the five words we live and play by, Leo,' Matias said.

Leo rattled them off. They were the words their father had drilled into them their whole life. 'Courtesy, integrity, perseverance, self-control, and indomitable spirit,' Leo said.

Jorge smiled. 'You are all those things and you have that spirit, Leo. It has been with you since you touched your first ball. There is no doubt my son – you are born to win. You are the *Pibe*.'

Leo flashed a grin, hugged his father tightly, and looked out the window once more at Barcelona. This would be his town now. His neighbourhood. His home. It was now up to him to prove his worth to FC Barcelona and the world.

★ ★ ★

When the loudspeaker called for boarding for flight 7767 to Buenos Aires, Leo kissed his mother, baby sister, and his brothers goodbye and watched them board the plane. Matias turned when he reached the door of the jumbo jet and held his hand up as if he were carrying a sword. Rodrigo joined him and Leo could almost see the tips of their swords touch. He held up his own imaginary sword towards them. 'All for one!' Matias and Rodrigo shouted to Leo.

'And one for all,' Leo shouted back.

Then Matias draped his arm over Rodrigo's shoulder and laughed and both boys spun on their heels and disappeared inside the plane.

Back on the terminal walkway, Leo let his imaginary sword slowly drop to his side and Jorge draped his arm over his shoulders and guided him away towards the exit and the car that was waiting for them. 'So, my son. Now that you are playing for Barça, how many goals will you score in your first year?'

Leo grinned. 'Plenty, Papa.'

When they reached the outside of the terminal, their driver Octavio jumped out of the car and opened the back door for them. Jorge climbed in and when Leo went to follow him, Octavio leaned down and whispered to him. 'I am also Argentine and Catalan. Some say you are the *Pibe*.'

Leo smiled at him. 'Papa, may I ride up front with Octavio? I want to hear all about Argentina,' he said, closed the back door, then turned to Octavio. 'As long as it is okay with you.'

'Sure!' said the driver.

Leo smiled and slid in. 'My friends call me Flea,' he said. Octavio flashed a big smile and closed the door. Leo relaxed in the front seat. They were going to pick up Leo's Spanish citizenship papers, and then go back to the hotel. There was much work to do before the first game. It was already March of 2001.

CHAPTER 18

SWEET HOME, ROSARIO

The morning is hot in Rosario as Celia holds tight
to Maria Sol's hand and they walk up the street.
Her hand keeps slipping out of Maria Sol's tiny
hand. Matias and Rodrigo walk ahead of them.
They are heading for the neighbourhood pitch so
Maria Sol can watch the children play. The sounds
of cheering and yelling and laughter fill the air and
Celia remembers when she could pick out Leo's
laughs from the others from a block away. When
they get to the pitch, Celia sees that some of the
boys wear Barça jerseys.

As the game continues, Matias and Rodrigo join
their mother and baby sister at the fence. Celia

feels her mother's spirit beside her. And when she looks out on the pitch, she imagines seeing Leo, the littlest kid on the team, charging towards the goal, faking the defender to the left, going right, and chipping the ball over the goalie's head, skimming it along the top of the net where it falls behind him, scoring a goal!

Celia checks her wristwatch and her eyes widen. 'It's almost time!' she says to the rest of her family. 'The match is about to start. Can you believe it? Leo is playing his first game for the A Team today!' Surrounded by her children, Celia hurries home to watch the match.

CHAPTER 19

WHAT DREAMS MAY COME

When Leo enters the Barça dressing room, the rest of the team is already there, suiting up. He approaches his locker with reverence. His name tops the list of Barça footballers that came before him. He opens the locker and dresses for the game. It is 1 May 2005, and earlier in the year, he proved himself to coach Frank Rijkaard in two previous games by winning a penalty and creating clear scoring chances. He is about to play his third game with the first team, this time against Albacete. He is only seventeen and the youngest player on the team.

A flash of orange and black runs by and slaps him

on the back. Leo looks up. It's his friend, Andrés Iniesta.

'Show time, Leo!' Andrés says.

Leo nods and leaps to his feet and follows his friends and teammates, Xavi, Andrés, and Ronaldinho out of the crowded dressing room.

The team tunnel to Camp Nou Stadium is long, its walls covered with gigantic portraits of the current FC Barcelona players. Leo trots proudly towards the light at the end and the stadium beyond, surrounded by his teammates. When they reach the end and enter into the stadium, the crowd erupts in a deafening roar. Leo's heart skips a beat. There are fans all around him and this time he crosses the sideline and makes his way to the centre for the Barça introductions. When he hears his name called, a chill runs down his back. He has dreamed of this moment his entire life.

Forty-four minutes later, Andrés throws in the ball and receives the return, dribbles easily past a few defenders and connects with Ronaldinho who lobs it over the last defender's head and right into Leo's path. Messi controls the ball perfectly, takes one more touch to ready himself and coolly chips the ball over the goalie straight into the side netting. He looks happy, then hears the whistle and sees the linesman's flag. Offside. Goal disallowed. Leo remains calm and smiles sheepishly. His first goal with the first team will have to wait.

Exactly one minute later, as if it were on instant replay, Ronaldinho once again lobs the ball over the defence. Leo calmly collects and again chips the ball right over the head of the keeper.

GOAL!!!

Leo jumps for joy, charges over to Ronaldinho and leaps on his back. As Ronaldinho races around the pitch, Leo raises his arms in the air. The crowd roars. Leo jumps down, raises his fingers towards heaven, and dedicates the first of many goals to his Grandma Celia, the woman who inspired him to get to this place.

On the sidelines, Coach Frank Rijkaard hugs his assistant, Pere Gratacós.

In the grandstands at the midline, Jorge Messi

leaps to his feet, cheers his son wildly, and kisses
the stranger next to him!

In the rows behind the coaches, Jose Maria
Minguella is on his feet, watching the boy perform
a miracle on the pitch. On the sidelines, Charly
Rexach puffs out his chest, proud of the boy from
Rosario.

In Rosario, and all over Argentina, fans and
families, Coach Apa and Mr Griffa, Gabriel
Digerolamo, Ernesto Vecchio and Carlos Morales,
Dr Schwartzstein, truck drivers and barge captains,
vegetable sellers and school teachers, future
footballers and normal schoolchildren are all on
their feet at once, screaming for joy in front of their
television sets as their own Leo Messi, the *Pibe*
from Rosario Argentina, scores his first goal for
Barça!

LIONEL MESSI HONOURS

Barcelona

★ La Liga (5): 2004–05, 2005–06, 2008–09, 2009–10, 2010–11

★ Copa del Rey (2): 2008–09, 2011–12;

★ UEFA Champions League (3): 2005–06, 2008–09, 2010–11

★ FIFA Club World Cup (2): 2009, 2011

Argentina

★ Olympic Gold Medal: 2008

★ FIFA U-20 World Cup: 2005

Individual

★ FIFA Ballon d'Or (3): 2010, 2011, 2012 (Created in 2010)

★ Ballon d'Or (1): 2009 (Ceased to exist in 2009

★ FIFA World Player of the Year (1): 2009 Ceased to exist in 2009

★ World Soccer Young Player of the Year (3): 2006, 2007, 2008

★ World Soccer Player of the Year (3): 2009, 2011, 2012

★ IFFHS World's Top Goal Scorer (2): 2011, 2012 [281]

★ Goal.com Player of the Year (2): 2009, 2011

★ El País King of European Soccer (4): 2009, 2010, 2011, 2012 [283]

★ ESPY Best International Athlete (1): 2012

★ European Golden Shoe (2): 2010, 2012

★ UEFA Best Player in Europe Award (1): 2011 (Created in 2011)

★ UEFA Club Footballer of the Year (1): 2009 (Ceased to exist in 2010)

★ UEFA Team of the Year (5): 2008, 2009, 2010, 2011, 2012

★ UEFA Champions League Top Goalscorer (4): 2009, 2010, 2011, 2012

★ UEFA Champions League Final Man of the Match (1): 2011

★ FIFA U-20 World Cup Player of the Tournament (1): 2005

★ FIFA Club World Cup Golden Ball (2): 2009, 2011

★ FIFA FIFPro World XI (6): 2007, 2008, 2009, 2010, 2011, 2012

★ FIFPro World Young Player of the Year (3): 2006, 2007, 2008

★ Pichichi Trophy (2): 2010, 2012

★ La Liga Player of the Year (3): 2009, 2010, 2011

★ La Liga Foreign Player of the Year (3): 2007, 2009, 2010 (Ceased to exist in 2010)

★ LFP Best Player (3): 2009, 2011, 2012 (No winner in 2010)

RECORDS

As of 10 February 2013

World

★ Most FIFA Ballon d'Or awards: 4

★ Guinness World Records title for the most goals in a year: 91 goals

★ Most international goals in a year (club and national team): 25 goals (shared with Vivian Woodward)

★ Most goals scored in FIFA Club World Cup: 4 goals (held jointly with Denilson Pereira Neves and Mohamed Aboutrika)

Europe

★ Most goals scored in a season (club): 73 goals

★ Most goals scored in a year (club): 79 goals

★ Most goals scored in a European Cup season: 14 goals (held jointly with José Altafini)

★ Most European Cup top scorer awards: 4 (shared with Gerd Müller)

★ Highest scorer in a European Cup game: 5 goals
   (held jointly with 10 other players)

Argentina

★ Most goals scored in a year (national team):
   12 goals (shared with Gabriel Batistuta)'

Spain

★ Most goals scored in La Liga in a season:
   50 goals
★ Most La Liga hat-tricks in a season: 8 hat-tricks
★ Most consecutive La Liga matches scored in:
   14 matches

Barcelona

★ Top scorer in official competitions: 301 goals
★ Top scorer in La Liga: 206 goals
★ Top scorer in UEFA Champions League: 56 goals
★ Top scorer in European competitions: 57 goals
★ Top scorer in international competitions: 61 goals
★ Most all competitions hat-tricks overall:
   22 hat-tricks
★ Most La Liga hat-tricks overall: 16 hat-tricks

BIBLIOGRAPHY

Caioli, Luca, *Messi: The Inside Story of the Boy Who Became a Legend* (Thriplow, Corinthian, 2010)

'Discovered: Interview with a 13-year-old Lionel Messi' (*Yahoo! Eurosport UK,* World of Sport, 19 October 2012; Web: 21 February 2013)

Ghosh, Bobby, 'Interview: Lionel Messi on His Sport, Cristiano Ronaldo, and Argentina' (*Time World,* 26 January 2012, Web: 21 February 2013)

Hunter, Graham, *Barca: The Making of the Greatest Team in the World* (United Kingdom, BackPage, 2012)

Ilongo, Sriram, 'The Lionel Messi Story: How Did He Get To The Top of The World?' (*Bleacher Report,* 16 August 2009; Web: 21 February 2013)

Kuper, Simon, *Soccer Men: Profiles of the Rogues, Geniuses, and Neurotics Who Dominate the World's Most Popular Sport* (New York, Nation, 2011)

'Lionel Messi: His Biography (English Subtitles) 2 Parts' (*YouTube*, 29 March 2011; Web: 21 February 2013)

'Lionel Messi Biography' (*Bio.com*, A&E Networks Television, n.d.; Web: 21 February 2013)

'Lionel Messi En Lima Peru' (*YouTube*, 17 January 2010; Web: 21 February 2013)

'Lionel Messi' (*Wikipedia*, Wikimedia Foundation, 21 February 2013; Web: 21 February 2013)

Logothetis, Paul, 'Messi's Rise with Barcelona Started on a Napkin' (*Home*. AP, 7 January 2012; Web: 21 February 2013)

Longman, Jeré, 'Boy Genius' (*The New York Times*, 22 May 2011; Web: 21 February 2013)

'Messi: From Scrawny Kid to History-maker' (*DAWN. com*, Reuters, 21 March 2012; Web: 21 February 2013)

'Messi 10', *Messi* (FC Barcelona, n.d.; Web: 21 February 2013)

Messi, Lionel, 'Leo Messi: My Life' (*Leo Messi Official Site*, Lionel Messi Foundation, n.d.; Web: 21 February 2013)

Papirblat, Schlomo, 'Growing Paean' (*Haaretz.com* 29 July 2011; Web: 21 February 2013)

'Red Bulletin', *Dream of the Pibe* (26 May 2010; Web: 21 February 2013)

Watt, Tom, *A Beautiful Game* (New York, Abrams, 2009)

'Young Lionel Messi at La Masia – FC Barcelona
More than a Club HD' (*YouTube*, 20 May 2011;
Web: 21 February 2013)